HOW GREAT PARENTS THINK

Written for busy parents of kids' ages up to 10

Straightforward Advice

Concrete Examples

Fun Activities

Written by Parents...for Parents!

James DeLuccia IV

To Loren, my family, Anderson, and Cooper Lu.
May they flourish in life.

CONTENTS

You are the best parent for your child

CHAPTER 1

THE SECRETS OF—AND THE HARD LESSONS FOR—PARENTS

ADVICE IN THIS CHAPTER

- ✓ Lessons and patterns
- ✓ Our scary privilege as parents
- ✓ How to connect emotionally with your child
- ✓ How you can use this book

- What attitudes and habits do we find in a good parent?
- How can you raise your child to experience the world more fully and more joyfully?
- What actions can you take now to set up your child for success in health, happiness, and their pursuits?
- As parents, what can we take away from studying the childhoods and the shared insights of global luminaries such as Elon Musk, Katrin Davidsdottir, Serena Williams, and Oprah Winfrey?

These are a sample of the questions we will answer throughout this text. Being a parent is not something you achieve; rather, it's something you become. A friend once said "anybody can be a father, but only with effort can you become her daddy." This, of course, holds true for a mother and mom. There is not a course or any hints on how to be a good parent, and at times, it can be a dark, scary, and lonely path. This text aims to alleviate some of that pain by teaching the attitudes and habits of exceptionally high performers so that you can apply these lessons to raising your child.

This book is perfect for any parent or soon to be parent, caregiver, and grandparent, whether mother, father, married, or single. This book speaks directly to challenges and journey for kids from 0-10 years old for families anywhere in the world. Whatever your place in life and aspirations for your child, the qualities and ways of thinking shared here will support you in those aspirations, as the lessons shared here are valuable to all.

The shared experiences draw from parents of only children to those with many children, boys, and girls. To keep the shared advice personal, the text will switch between speaking about girls and boys, and we will alternate between using the pronouns "she" and "he." However, regardless of the gender of the child described in a specific story, please adopt any advice you can for your family. On that note, don't be afraid to read both the boy and girl chapters! Many readers have gleaned nuggets of wisdom from reading about raising the opposite gender than only the sex-specific chapter about their child. Remember, you are not raising your child in a vacuum. At the very least, these chapters will give you the insights necessary to deal with the boys and girls who are sharing your child's life, and therefore of importance to you.

Being a good parent is not woven into your genes, where you either have good parenting genes or not. The qualities and ways of thinking can be learned, and that is what this book is about.

WHY THIS MATTERS

Thus far, you and others have relied on instinct and assumed that all of the experts were right, that you must follow their very detailed advice or you would fail. This text combines key insights, concrete examples, research, and parental experience, all in the hopes that you can use what is covered in these pages to better our future generation of leaders, heroes, and inventors.

LESSONS AND PATTERNS—LIKE NOTHING YOU'VE SEEN BEFORE

There are distinct opportunities in your child's life that will shape her entire existence. You have the ability to nurture her to become confident, polite, athletic, and knowledgeable. Kids are who they are, and as parents, we have the chance to cultivate their strengths. They soak up our words, actions, and behaviors. Our children, like us, are seeking lessons and patterns. This is how they learn to survive in the world—for better or worse. As parents, we must be nimble and mindful of children's unique personalities, just as we must remain responsible and conscious of the example we set for them.

Unlike all other texts on this topic, the content here identifies key behaviors you can adopt now. Some are fun and playful, others are simply preparing you with the right drugs in case of a cold, and others address the right amount of TV/reading/play that led to our most admired public officials.

This is not an instruction guide, but a tool for you to apply to your own mannerisms to enable your daughter or son to succeed in this world.

OUR PRIVILEGE AS PARENTS

You have the greatest gift in the world: a child. It truly is a miracle of nature that her birth was possible, and a privilege granted to you as her parent. It is compelling that we are one of the rare species that must care for our young for so long before they are able to survive independently. Humans have excelled on our planet as the dominant species due to our endless efforts to share our knowledge with one generation to the next[1]. As a result, the ability for future generations to build upon what we have created is extraordinary. It is parents' privilege to share what we have learned throughout our lifetimes, much like our parents shared with us and their parents shared with them. This constant betterment of the human condition is truly evolution at its best.

---

1 Harari, Yuval N. Sapiens: A Brief History of Humankind. , 2015. Print.

It is a privilege to care for your child. As you muster the strength and courage each morning, night, and in between, *focus on this privilege.* Realize that you don't have to perform these duties for your child; rather you GET TO do these things for her.

- You GET TO take your son to school
- You GET TO read her a story
- You GET TO make dinner with him

The trouble is, you think you have time.
- Buddha

Time is not only what is most important; it is all that matters. Cherish it. Take advantage of every chance you have to be with your little one. Your child will grow, learn, and change every minute of every day. If you are gone or not paying attention—you will miss it. Worse, you miss teaching and growing with your child. Consider changing your life to maximize your time together:

- Take all the leave time your employer allows immediately after birth.
- Wake up for every feeding (or every other one, to remain sane).
- Travel? Find ways to be home more often.
- Commute for 2-4 hours a day? Find ways to rework your schedule so you are home when she is awake.
- Need to work late? Consider being home when she is awake and working evenings AFTER she has gone to bed.
- Need to work weekends? Wake up a few hours before her and get it done.

Do whatever it takes, because time will pass and these opportunities to spend quality time together will dwindle. The key is that this time be maximized for quality—being present, engaged with the child, and 100% focused without multi-tasking with phones, computers, and busyness.

Luminary Highlight: Adversity and Challenge are common theme to our generation's' greats

Elon Musk, Richard Branson, Bethenny Frankel, Oprah Winfrey, and many other each had difficult childhoods and challenges in their childhood. While alone these do not make these individuals great, but they do demonstrate the value in allowing our children to be challenged and give them the room to try, fail, endure, and try again[1].

What a wonderful world it would be if we can use these challenges to bring an up swell of venturous spirited leaders in the next generation without the need for the abuse, pain, and battles these luminaries had to personally face[2].

1   "Why Childhood Adversity Creates Great Entrepreneurs – Medium." 24 Mar. 2015, https://medium.com/@JasonShuman/why-childhood-adversity-creates-great-entrepreneurs-9b1ce015f06a. Accessed 12 Dec. 2016.

2   "Elon Musk Worries That His Kids Are Too Soft To Be Entrepreneurs ...." 16 Sep. 2011, http://www.businessinsider.com/elon-musk-worries-that-his-kids-are-too-soft-to-be-entrepreneurs-2011-9. Accessed 12 Dec. 2016.

HOW TO USE THIS BOOK

Read it straight through or jump around based on your current situation. Whatever reading style you choose, use it as a reference guide over the next few years as your child grows. The advice contained here was gathered based on powerful behaviors and lessons. It is intentionally brief and direct. This is not for those interested in the science; that is saved for other, more detailed texts that were part of this book's research. This is for the mother or father who is seeking immediate, concrete, situational answers.

The research discussed here, as well as the quotes and takeaways from public figures, are meant to provide a foundation. Life requires flexibility, but a general path is needed, too. The following chapters provide that path, should you choose to take it.

Of course, this book does not contain all the answers. That would be impossible. Instead, it offers tactics and tips to guide you through many situations. While we cannot prepare you for all of the curve balls thrown your way, we will teach you how to think like a great parent, so that when the time comes to make your own unique and personal decisions, you will have the wisdom and compassion of many great parents who came before you.

While I have been exploring the life of a parent these past years, I can't overstate that these collections were a community effort. From extensive interviews, online surveys, deep online research, and professionals in the field support have pushed this content beyond its initial conception. Without this group effort, this book would not be what is today.

YOU HAVE EVERYTHING YOU NEED TO BE A GREAT PARENT

You are the best parent for your child, and while there will be moments of doubt and regret on how you address a situation, you have the chance of a lifetime. There is no upper limit to what your child can accomplish and the happiness you both can realize. Set your aspirations high and make them limitless for your child. No life situation can prevent your child from achieving the most ambitious of goals. Know that, and parent in such a manner. The hundreds of ideas in this book will support you on this journey, but you need to apply them and know that there are no limits. Let your imagination guide you allow you to connect to every child. Just as there is an incredible future ahead for your child, there is an incredible future in store for you as her parent.

Our imagination cannot help but travel to the places these children live

- Pope Francis[2]

---

2   Pope Francis, Dear Pope Francis: The Pope Answers Letters from Children Around the World, Loyola Press February 1, 2016.

CHAPTER 2

KEYS TO THE HEART AND SOUL OF YOUR DAUGHTER

SECRETS IN THIS CHAPTER:
- ✓ Emotions
- ✓ Nails, hair, and all things nice
- ✓ The journey, not the destination

Girls are wonderful gifts to the world. They seek to make things beautiful, colorful, and joyful. From the day they are born and as they grow into their own personalities, they are incredible. As a daddy to a boisterous and curious daughter, I am privileged to have my entire world transformed by her grace and courage. She has forever changed my understanding of women and the impact they bring to the world. My hope for this chapter is to highlight what mothers already know deeply, and uncover the opportunity for fathers to learn from the females in our lives.

The insights within this chapter are drawn from a broad spectrum of resources, including a collection of research ranging from early childhood specialists to exceptional parents to general surveys on parenting. The intent here is to be practical and set up scenarios that will enable you to grow with your daughter.

Children spell LOVE

T–I–M–E

Emotions

She is full of emotions. She does not fully understand what she is feeling, how to interpret them, or how to react. We may have thousands of words to describe all of the emotions we experience, but few of us really understand all of them. Imagine how confusing this must be for a child, and eventually, for a young lady!

As you connect with your daughter, recognize her potential. To be a good parent, you must emanate emotional maturity, engage her, and be proud as she becomes attuned to her emotions. The ideas here can be shared with sons too, but we must recognize that the male brain and the female brain are different. How girls see the world and how they approach it is very different from the way in which boys do, and thus the idea of two unique chapters.

USE ABSOLUTE WORDS

Speak to your daughter with emotion. Be absolute in your meaning—absolutely positive or absolutely negative. It is not possible, in her mind, for you to have two favorite colors; you can have only one. Do you LOVE that picture? Do you LOVE spaghetti? You must take a position and speak in absolute terms.

Do not worry, you are not forever bound to one position, but it is important that you are honest. Society has encouraged us to be politically correct, but this is not necessarily the best thing for your daughter. You should give yourself—and her—the freedom to have a definite opinion.

When an argument emerges between you and your daughter, it is important to use emotional words to enhance her understanding of the issue. If she harmed you or another, you should express it in age appropriate emotions. Explain to her, "I am SAD that you did X; it hurt my feelings." (Notice the statement of the feelings as well as the result of those feelings.) While this technique allows her to better understand her world around her, keep in mind that this is a powerful and significant statement in her mind. Always mean what you say, and do not use these emotional expressions lightly.

It is especially important to hold your ground. If you are sad, resolve it with her; do not ignore it or allow it to be dismissed. Remember you are driving the development of her personality, and this situation is a perfect teaching moment. We wish to develop our children's social skills and our own coping skills. If we drop or dismiss these emotional moments, she will never create the appropriate learned behaviors. As a great parent reinforced with me, *if you subsidize it [bad behavior]; it will grow.*

HUG HONESTLY

A hug is an important gesture that should be cherished, as it gives you a chance to connect with, and show your heart to, your daughter. When you hug, do it honestly, powerfully, longingly, and with love. It matters, and she is worth it. Every damn time.

There is no remedy for love than to love more
- David Thoreau

Nails, hair, and all things nice

Girls love pretty things. This means that color, sparkles, glitter, and especially art will be deeply important to your daughter. The desire to create art, drawings, and "pretty things" (even if they are ugly) will be a pursuit of most girls. You will see that through this art, their ability to create, express themselves, and mirror their love is amazingly personal. As your child gains more fine motor skills, she'll begin to see her own skin, hair, and accessories (bracelets, rings, necklaces, hair items) as a medium for this expression. As such, your personal time together will begin to include richer forms of expression, such as painting nails and doing hair. Embrace these creative ventures and allow her own self to blossom.

For the moms and grandmas, you have a wonderful advantage when engaging your child on these activities, and you will find great joy reliving early memories. Much of this chapter may seem simple, but there are gems for you, too. For the dads and grandpas, these notes and ideas are for you to help you along. You can make it happen, and your daughter will love you for it.

PAINT THE NAILS

Painting nails is often favorite activity of the little ladies as they see adults with colorful, sparkly nails. The desire to emulate is a powerful force.

You must paint her nails. It may take 30 minutes and she may fall asleep while you do it, but you must. At first, they will not be pretty. You will spend a ton of time cleaning up, but that will not matter for long. Every time she looks at her nails, she will think of the deep attention you gave to her and the great care you took when painting her nails, and to every kid and adult she sees, her nails and how YOU painted them will be a topic of pride.

You'll need a few simple things, all available on Amazon or at your local convenience store:

- Nail polish (Small bottles are fun because they are usually bright. Bonus: if you spill, you will make a smaller mess).
- Q-tips, cotton swabs (to use in cleanup).
- Nail polish remover (it stinks but it works).
- Newspaper or magazines to put under her hands while you paint.
- Paper towels, for a variety of reasons. Better to have them than not.

That is it—have fun and paint away! Check out YouTube if you really want to get aggressive with your art.

DO THE HAIR

Girl hair is fun and can be made into "crazy hair day" very easily. It is also the worst tangled Christmas light nightmare you have ever seen if you are not mindful. So respect the hair and learn to care for it.

Washing her hair can be a fun bonding experience and a bit soapy with a soaking now and again. For the dads washing hair, take care to be thorough and use conditioner. You'll find almost no knots when brushing her hair later on.

Brushing wet hair should involve some type of de-tangling comb; a brush or comb is fine for dry hair. This will help free the hair of knots and reduce the chance of a serious meltdown. These meltdowns occur because pulling of hair hurts, a lot. Especially if you pull only a few hairs at a time. Brush in short strokes, hold her head steady, and work the tangled pieces out in parts. Remember, that hair is attached to her sensitive, little skull!

Pro-tip
These baths/showers often happen at the latest part in the day when she is most tired, so keep your patience, be gentle, and firmly move through the process.

BRAIDS!

Never braided hair before? Never made a ponytail before? Good, now you get to learn something new! It will be a daily part of her life, and there is no reason you cannot learn. If you can tie your shoes, you can learn to braid hair like a pro.

Search YouTube for visual step by step guides online:
- Ponytails
- Braids
- French braids

Single father?
Use YouTube and get it done.

Full Household?
Have someone teach you, but don't allow them to "let me show you," i.e., see you screwing up and take over for you. That is a cop out, and you are not a quitter.

DO ALL THE STUFF!

You are not too old, too important, and damn well not too scared, to get on the ground with your little one and engage her. Overcome your limitations so you do not subconsciously instill them in your child!

Never good reasons:	Transform yourself:
1. Too busy	1. Let's do it!
2. I have work	2. I'll work when you sleep
3. Ask your mother	3. Let's do it together
4. I don't know how	4. Let's figure it out
5. I am scared	5. For you, I shall overcome

There are so many great things you can do together and a huge world you can introduce her to at home. A few of my favorites include:

- Teaching headstands
- Playing catch
- Making airplanes
- Balloon volleyball
- Costumes/dress up
- Building a fort with pillows and blankets or umbrellas
- Gymnastics (flips, cartwheels, etc.)
- Yoga

Remember this a journey and not a destination. If you do not have a certain skill, no problem—you can learn it with your child, together. How wonderful to get quality time AND learn a new skill. So get upside down, learn the headstand, and stand at the edge of life with your daughter.

THE FUTURE BELONGS TO THOSE WHO BELIEVE IN THE BEAUTY OF THEIR DREAMS.

ELEANOR ROOSEVELT

The Journey is the Destination

Raising a girl is certainly a marathon and not a sprint, and while this is obvious with years of perspective, it also applies to the little moments. This is a key insight into the mind of your little girl. When you are engaged in any activity (example below), it is more about experiencing the process and less about completing it. This ties into the psychology of our child, shared Dr. Kaywork, a specialist in early childhood development, where girls compose a mental plan, while our sons are more about just doing it ad-hoc.

To put it simply, we are not on a mission to finish the task as quickly as possible. Instead, focus on the details. If we are painting, set up the right paint and simply paint for the joy of painting. There is no perfect, finished painting, and it may often be repainted or painted over to continue the experience.

TAKE DOLLS TO THE BEACH

FUN IS IN THE PREPARATION & TRAVEL

In the above example, if we rushed getting to the beach and did not explore the richness of the process, we would have missed the whole point and all the fun. It is in these playtime activities that you will help your daughter build a foundation on which to prepare for the world. Topics that are directly or indirectly raised in these play sessions can include lifelong lessons. Some you can craft, while others simply provide direction and allow her to form her own opinions.

For example:

If we are playing with Barbie and the plan is to have them assemble their friends to go to the beach (across the room), then the joy is in (listed in priority order, according to her perspective):

1. The discussion of Barbie's friends going to the beach
2. The outfits of those going
3. The creative way they are getting to the beach
4. Who is traveling in which car to the beach
5. Where everyone is sitting
6. What everyone is bringing
7. Packing everything
8. Talking through fun and fear between dolls on trip
9. Actually going to the beach
10. Getting to the beach

More often than not, as soon as everything is unpacked at the beach one of two things will happen: you will have a fun play time at the beach, or more often in my case, it will "rain" and everyone will go back to the house and start a new game.

TOPICS YOU MAY BE COME ACROSS:

- Bullying—whether your daughter is the victim or the bully
- Selfishness vs selflessness
- Being mean versus kind

- Death
- Marriage (usually love is what she means)
- Kissing
- Cliques
- Divorce
- Racism
- Stereotypes (girls do X or can't do Y)

It is your job as the parent not just to keep playtime, but also to improve the story in the games you are playing. Oftentimes you will get to do this in character while playing, but sometimes you will to have to break character and create a change in the attitudes and behaviors of the toys.

The use of these toys allows safe exploration of ideas and concerns of your girl. Embrace this time to enjoy playing, and be actively engaged in the open, raw, and safe management of tough topics.

> *It is your job as the parent not just to keep playtime, but also to improve the story in the games you are playing.*

BE ANYTHING

The imagination of your little girl is unlimited. She will envision worlds that don't exist, create rich stories between the simplest and most complex toys available, and make herself a participant in these worlds. This is the space where she can try and do anything, and it is also where her passions shine brightest.

Encourage and support these rich dreams, as they set the foundation on which she'll pursue her hobbies. They also will give you a sneak peek into areas where she is naturally gifted. For instance, as a child, Oprah Winfrey entertained herself by "playacting" in front of an "audience" of farm animals. At the age of 2, she even addressed her church congregation about "when Jesus rose on Easter Day.[3]" It is in these areas where we as parents in the long run support our girl's passions and sometimes, not always, accept her being average at academics.

Freedom, independence, safety, space, and support are all that our children need to create these imaginary worlds. In fact, up to the age of a toddler, two to three items are more than enough (any more and these are likely to be ignored or lost) to create these rich worlds. The magic of this free play and pretend world is simple—there are no limits, no risk, and only possibilities. The spirit and energy of this world can be seen viscerally by adults around the time of Christmas and Easter with the ideas of Santa Claus and the Easter Bunny. Speak to your girl to understand her passion and perhaps some of that magic will reinvigorate you too.

Oh the places your girl will go, and if you let her, she'll take you too[4]. An endearing part of your little girl's imagination is her unlimited ability to do and become anything. This may mean building a castle, a home, or a city with Legos, blocks, or Tupperware, and then having a full life story unfold with characters. She may make a rocket or train and then act as an astronaut or engineer. There are no limits and as she grows from late infant to early childhood her games and imagination will change based on her experiences. Playing school will be powerful, because there are actual limits imposed on her at school and not in imagination. There will also be a strong frequency of mimicking your activities—talking on the phone; going on trips; being a teacher, and even your home "chores" (sweeping, vacuuming, and such).

Let her be anything. Support her imagination. Participate in her make believe worlds, and keep the play simple. Too often parents (guys especially) try to add in too much complexity, characters, items, and such into the play world. She doesn't require such materialistic items, but instead your time, participation, and company on her journey.

---

3   "Oprah Winfrey Biography - life, family, childhood, parents, name, story ...." http://www.notablebiographies.com/We-Z/Winfrey-Oprah.html. Accessed 13 Dec. 2016.

4   Seuss, Dr. Oh, the Places You'Ll Go! New York :Random House, 1990. Print.

BE PRESENT

There is nothing greater than connecting authentically with your daughter. She will love you to levels that can scare and strengthen you as a parent. The only requirement is that you be present—meaning you have made time where your undivided purpose is to engage her. Being present is the act of mindfully living and maximizing the current activity—not planning the next one, mentally making a shopping list, checking a phone, or sneaking an eye to the TV. Being present is a practice with its roots in Buddhist philosophy and other meditative traditions, which teaches experiencing reality "as is"[5]. Mindfulness cultivates conscious attention and awarness of the moment in a non-judgmental way[6].

Time is the one thing we can never get back or redo. Make the time. You have a finite amount of time with her; she is awake for only a few hours every day. Once you take school out, this time is about three to four hours a day together, and it is your privilege to spend time with her. All else can be done once she is asleep.

Being present is harder in this age of mobile phones and the pressure to be connected all the time. If you want to be a good parent, you MUST be emotionally and mentally present. Here are some ways to give her your undivided attention:

- No phones during playtime
- No phones or tablets at tea parties
- Stop doing chores/cooking/other adult activity when she wants to play
- Turn off the TV

Life happens and we as adults must do things (work, bills, dinner, etc.) that have to be done. While work at home parents who are

---

5   Kabat-Zinn, J. (1990). Full catastrophe living. How to cope with stress, pain and illness using mindfulness meditation. London: Piatkus.

6   Passmore,J.,& Marianetti, O. (2013). The role of mindfulness in coaching. The Coaching Psychologist. 3(3), 131-138

raising kids must too get the job done, a balance is vital and must be equitable. There is a fine line between teaching your child that you can be both a great stay at home parent while working, and being a poor parent.

Being present as a practice applies to our work, other family members, the public, and our children. As we demonstrate an honest desire to connect in each interaction, we teach our child that everyone deserves that connection, too. Many times, it requires us to ignore, silence, or put away those gadgets because in the end, you and I both know that the Facebook post you were going to write is not worth missing a moment with your child.

Being physically present is not the same as BEING present and something that can accidentally slip away. As you seek to practice and demonstrate being 100% present with your child, include them actively in the process! A practice that a great parent and specialist in early childhood development shared was the act of reading and discussing mindfulness and meditation. This topic can be raised simply through books, shared discussion, meditation, yoga, and art. Seek out what is best for your home to set an environment that fosters the warmth and love that our children cherish.

There are many benefits tied to practicing mindfulness and even short mediation activities for people of all ages. Research has shown impressive benefits for teens through adults. The better we can instill being mindful and present for our children, the more likely they'll also benefit now and throughout their life. The general agreement across the available peer reviewed articles is that many skills improved including[7]:

---

7   "A Longitudinal Study of Students' Perceptions of Using Deep Breathing Meditation to Reduce Testing Stresses", Ginal Paul, Barb Elam, Steven Verhulst. Teaching and Learning Online,Published online June 2007.

- Decreased test anxiety, nervousness, and self-doubt[8]
- Longer attention span and improves concentration[9]
- Improved self-regulation
- Better social–emotional perception

In the research and articles which were more conceptual in nature, the authors all proposed that children experience positive outcomes including:

- Increased happiness
- Self-awareness
- Stress reduction[10]

8   "Mindfulness based stress reduction for medical students: optimising student satisfaction and engagement". Declan Aherne, Katie Farrant, Louise Hickey, Emma Hickey, Lisa McGrath, Deirdre McGrath

9   "Study Suggests Meditation Can Help Train Attention - The New York ...." 8 May. 2007, http://www.nytimes.com/2007/05/08/health/psychology/08medi.html. Accessed 13 Dec. 2016.

10   Elizabeth J. Erwin & Kimberly A. Robinson (2015): The joy of being: making way for young children's natural mindfulness, Early Child Development and Care, DOI: 10.1080/03004430.2015.1029468

"

TREAT A CHILD AS THOUGH HE IS ALREADY THE PERSON HE'S CAPABLE OF BECOMING "

- HAIM GINOTT

A SCHOOL TEACHER, A CHILD PSYCHOLOGIST AND PSYCHOTHERAPIST AND A PARENT EDUCATOR.

CHAPTER 3

KEYS TO THE HEART AND SOUL OF YOUR SON

SECRETS IN THIS CHAPTER:
- ✓ Experiences
- ✓ Character

Boys are different from girls and distinctly unique from each other boy. Physical space is required to allow their energy to be applied and expressed. While your daughter will be balls of energy inside and outside, boys are on a whole other level. As one parent described to me—"we thought our house was kid proof, until we had a son and things began to rattle and shake!"

Embracing their unique spirits and joining them as they blossom through their growth spurts will be your greatest joy. The shared ideas and habits within here are from highly successful parents and will help you setup fun and engaging moments with your boys for the first ten years.

Experiences

Your son, like daughters, will seek out activities and new experiences. As you venture and introduce the world to your boy, please take a deep breath. Boys need to figure things out on their own and will try to do something in a manner you may not have considered. Patience will be your ally—both patience in allowing your boy to plot his own course and patience in allowing him to make mistakes that require the effort to be retried. In our research on this chapter, this patience is one aspect that resonated consistently as the hallmark of developing independence and a happy home.

BOYS DON'T SIT STILL

The space to express themselves—the room to move, throw, toss, jump, roll, sprint, dodge, mix, build, and break—is required for every boy. From an early age, boys will be active and begin to move faster, harder, with greater mass AND with swinging objects as they move into early childhood (and beyond if we really think about it).

As the parent, you need to let them be boys, and allow for lessons best taught through rough housing, exploring in yards/fields, and physical contact. During this growth, you as the adult need to instill respect, balance, and strength in your child. As your son's skill extends to greater activities as well as more remote and independent play, you'll need them to have the skills and your trust.

You can create these spaces and moments to develop his character in the following examples:

- Create a room (such as a basement) with no breakables for boy play where they are free to explore their creativity and express themselves without too many rules.
- Institute clear and specific rules on what games can be played where, such as no running indoors; no throwing/shooting in the dining room, etc.

- Team sports—get them involved and grow their passion. These group activities will help develop precision to their fine motor skills, as well as teach them how to properly and safely interact with other boys.
- Give them goals to focus their non-stop energy and perhaps limit 'parenting moments.'

You want to direct the energy that is swelling in your son. Give him tools, activities, space, and encouragement to use that energy for as long as he desires (which will be sun up to sundown, in case you were wondering).

IMAGINATION ABOVE ALL

Amazement with our physical world and all that is possible in it is the space of boys. You'll find a deep-rooted passion about anything that drives, flies, and floats. Even a few small toys (which could be simply three small blocks of wood pretended to be cars) can entertain and envelope your son for long spans of time. Children don't need much, but they LOVE props for their play and even a few small ones can help them immerse themselves into this big world they see all around.

The more we can do to encourage and allow this exploration and play through imagination, the better. As your little boy moves from toddler to early childhood, you'll find that the toy's adventures will be grander, that there will most likely will be battles against good and evil, and you'll likely lose some key kitchen utensils in the adventures.

Super powers!! From the moment after age three, boys (well into their late 80s) enjoy and believe in super powers. The ideas of accomplishing greatness with beyond this world's abilities are the seeds of inspiration and greatness. These imaginations lead people to believe they can get to space, fly to Mars, and make electric cars. Sometimes super powers become real life, and as parents, all we can do is encourage these imaginations, aspirations, and experiences. Never should we limit their vision for the possible, and who knows? Maybe one day you'll be helping them set a path to achieve that goal.

Here are a few toys to engage with them and then step away as the parent:

- Legos (bigger size up to age four is ideal, as boys will eat a few for sure (Great because you can build a few things together if they come in a kit, and then your son can then play with this on their own afterwards!)
- Matchbox cars
- Train cars
- Boats
- Any fire, police, medical vehicles. (These are awesome because they come in all sorts of forms, ranging from trucks to helicopters to boats. Even better? The people in the vehicles are real life heroes.)
- Superheroes of the Marvel and DC comic book universes (your son will become a fan of these usually as TV, movies, and cinema enter their life)

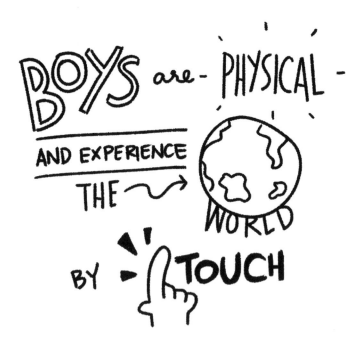

GET DIRTY

It's gross? Fun! There's dirt? Who cares! Boys like to make a mess, and puddles, food, and just about anything else is fair game. Boys are physical and experience the world by touch. There is also little fear, zero hesitation, and nearly no concept of "off limits"—that includes their penis. Their exploration of the world will lead to a great deal of mess and dirt. That is just part of the journey.

- Rain outside → Great puddles and mud to play in!
- Dirt pile → Awesome! Let's make a fort with our hands!
- Poop → Funny subject for jokes and drawing!

Have clean wipes, a spare change of clothes (shoes too), a towel, and a suitcase of patience. Appreciate that this is your son exploring the world. Certainly we can limit and steer them in some situations (rules rules!), but they are boys and boys happen.

BE CLEAN

Boys are far simpler on clothes, dressing, and managing through what is weather appropriate than girls are. You are lucky here. Clothing is simply pants/shorts and a t-shirt. Any and all combinations will do. Throughout interviews with parents, they each shared the uphill battle of ensuring their boys changed all of their dirty clothes, so keep an eye out for this parenting duty. Funny, it has only been in the last couple hundred years that washing regularly became the norm. Boys today are perhaps from a prior century![11]

Actively participating and helping your son be clean will be a role for you. Teaching them how to shower, how to groom themselves, and how to change all of their clothes will be necessary. Note: this is a stark difference to girls who are more likely to change their full outfit twice a day with absolutely no provocation other than "I wanted to wear this outfit right now."

---

11   Harari, Yuval N. Sapiens: A Brief History of Humankind. , 2015. Print.

Cleanliness will help keep your home free of mud footprints and reduce rashes and illnesses from your children. A win-win, as all of these will be equally rough for you the parent as they are for your boy.

Character

What makes up a man but the sum of his experiences in life? As you share every precious moment with your son, consider this and enjoy the process of building his character. This means helping him understand and manage his emotions (yes, boys have emotions too, though they usually fall in the happy/sad/ mad category). Furthermore, you must help him learn to rise to the challenges placed before him.

Boys can be expressive across the spectrum of emotion and while some may be very sensitive, others can be completely free spirits. The way you navigate these waters will be unique, but there are areas where you can instruct and steer your boy.

RAISE A GENTLEMAN

As boys grow into their own self, the manners, habits, and lessons you have instilled and demonstrated with them will become evident. Many great parents discuss how they raise their boys with the image of a gentleman. They live these habits in their own house with each other—"gentleman" is a label simply capturing a set of characteristics that boys and girls can possess.

To raise a gentleman, you must first accept and embrace this is a journey and not a "21 Day Transformation" so common in our current society. We are not merely seeking to teach; rather we are aiming to adopt daily habits that, as they are mimicked by our child, will lead to the summation of a gentleman. Key habits highlighted by our research and examples from great parents are included below. I challenge you to continue these practices yourself, and to find new ways to help your boy grow his character.

- **Look everyone in the eye when they speak** - this is a powerful way of demonstrating authentic connection and gives confidence to the speaker. This is taught by example by the parent to both adults and kids, and is a fantastic way of halting kids interrupting discussions. (As they will realize, when it is their turn to speak they will also not be interrupted by another kid, adult, or phone.)

- **"Please" and "Thank you"** - every time for everyone.
- **"You are welcome" and "my pleasure"** - You delivering the emotional gratitude reinforces the authenticity and provides a positive feedback loop for the behavior.
- **Handwritten notes of gratitude** - There are many moments when you and your child can write a note for someone. These instances are best done on paper, by hand, and if possible with a bias towards creativity. Great moments include:
  » Birthdays
  » Seasonal Cards
  » Thank you cards (ex: when a gift is received, have your child and you write thank you cards BEFORE using/playing with item. It shows respect and associates two positive activities together.)
- **Help others** - Instilling a civic and human duty to protect and come to the aid of those in need is a powerful character trait. This requires you to teach when such help is right to be given, and for whom. Some situations you'll encounter and must teach around:
  » Standing up for a friend from a bully
  » Defending another child from harm
  » Advocating for others and themselves
  » Carrying heavy loads
  » Assisting those in need
- **Respect girls** - Ladies can be very strong, but the fact is the strongest woman is still physically weaker than the strongest man. Therefore, we need to instill a level of respect for girls. Beyond strength, by age ten the ideas of sexual jokes, behaviors, and experiences will be in the conversation. Establishing respect early will provide better discussions.
- **Respect effort** - Teach our children and boys to not be busy and to do work, but respect effort. Teaching them to respect the process athletes, professionals, and others put forward to achieve an accomplishment will associate value in winning fairly. This will

also embed the idea that with effort they too can accomplish their wildest ambitions.

Great Parent Tip: Advocating and defending others, a high road that is not without bumps

"The world ain't all sunshine and rainbows. It's a very mean and nasty place, and I don't care how tough you are. It will beat you to your knees and keep you there permanently if you let it."
- Rocky Balboa, 2006

To be a gentleman, to be a responsible person, and to be a reliable friend is not easy. Your boy will find difficult situations where he believes the right action is to defend someone, to advocate against a bully, and fight against the "group think." You as the parent must give them the confidence that you support their actions and that you will be there to support them if another action must be taken. The confidence this gives your child is undeniable. It will help them in school, sports and in the future when they face the real world. If you don't allow them to do this, they will never learn. (Stacey O.)

NAVIGATING FRIENDSHIPS

The tribe your boy runs with will heavily influence his activities, behavior, and education. Where we live, our neighborhood streets, and our extracurricular activities all contribute to our boy's group of friends. If you live in a neighborhood full of kids near the same age, you are lucky and should embrace free kid play. If not, athletic or after school programs are very good at building these friend circles. Ideally, these activities will be in the same school district, so that these relationships will begin to feed and build as the children progress in the school system.

At a certain age, you'll begin hearing stories of "bad kids" from your son. You'll hear about disagreements and the like. While you need to instill a skill of self-managing, you also need to develop his ability to navigate friendships, where "navigate" means to identify those children who are good friends and those who are not. Teaching your child to evaluate their friends is not easy, but habits from great parents include:

- Teaching that "good friends" are the children who play fair and don't hurt.
- Instilling that bullies require your son to stand up and advocate for himself or another friend—although this is difficult, our sons must take first step towards conflict resolution.
- The 'true friend test'—those who will be standing by your side when you are in trouble, and who would they stand by in a similar situation.
- Teaching our children to always be nice to others, even if we don't have anything in common today, is important, as they might develop similar interests down the road.

Pressure to like and dislike kids is strong starting at a very early age. As the parent, you can encourage your child to measure and make friends based on what they believe is right and good. Building your boy's character to navigate these complex relationships will be valuable. As the character of your child develops and their position of right and wrong strengthens, they will be able to go against the masses, protect those in need, and do good.

BE PRESENT

This is so important it bears repeating and restatement for both girls and boys. There is nothing greater than connecting authentically with your son. He will love you for it, and the bonds you build of trust, respect, and attachment will equally strengthen you and him. Boys are much more physical and practicing being present will also save a few broken electronics too!

Soon your boy will be spending every day of the week from 7

A.M.–4 P.M. at school and then running with friends. The small bit of time you have together is brief already, and letting it slip due to a lack of time, or worse, lack of quality time is something you'll never make up. Seize these playful moments and get dirty with your son. As a parent to a young boy, you can enjoy being a player in his games, but ultimately you'll become a spectator. How you parent and teach your child is defined at an early age in one-on-one activity.

Being present is harder in this age of mobile phones and the pressure to be connected all the time. If you want to be a good parent is more than just being physically present—that is a "D-" on the grading scale. You MUST be mentally and physically present. Here are some ways to be present:

- No phones during playtime
- No phones or tablets nearby or part of game
- Stop doing chores/cooking/other adult activity when playing
- Turn off the TV
- Lace up the old shoes and get in the dirt
- Lose the dry cleaning/delicate clothing and get rowdy and hands-on

Life happens, and we as adults must do things (work, bills, dinner, etc.) that have to be done. As we achieve a balance, where we are focused on each task, we ultimately also teach our son the value of hard work, engaging with people by looking them in the eyes, and that sometimes it requires them to not be the center of attention. As for those smartphones and gadget notifications, you and I both know that Facebook post is not worth it.

> **Great Parenting Practice: Being present early pays dividends in the teen years for family**
>
> Stacey, a mother in a family of boys, highlighted the following benefit that emerged when her boys grew older:
>
> "Being present and engaging with our kids (boys for us) has led to building a trusting relationship when they got older. It allowed for open lines of communication and trust as they begin navigating middle and high school, where they have access to a lot more information, situations, and difficult moments. I expect they will have questions, they will have issues...and we have ensured that our door is always open for them to walk through, and together we can tackle the important topics."
>
> Stacey notes that topics her family has already discussed include—bullying, sex, race, drugs, and cheating.

WIN

Winning matters. Everything is and can be made into a competition. Fastest down stairs; fastest up the hill; most somersaults; quickest to finish breakfast; throw the farthest; highest test score; fastest at saying the alphabet, who (wins) gets to be the captain and pick the kickball team, and on it goes.

Your boy will create many competitions and this is natural. Competition will happen between all of the toys and even with you. How you react, participate, and win matters. The good guys don't always win. The one who is most gifted doesn't always win. The one who works the hardest doesn't always win, and your son doesn't win every time.

We highlight winning and losing a few times across the book, as it was reinforced across many parent experiences and is so vital. As the parent, you can create an environment that encourages competitions and treats them as fairly as possible. Your reaction to wins and losses will be mimicked by your child. So enjoy the wins, cherish the losses, and at the end be sure everyone gets a high-five and a hug before heading in.

EMOTIONS

Yes, your son has them. Though universes different from girls, they still exist. Engaging and helping them accept their feelings is important for parents, but it is also important not to dwell on them. Boys have three states—happy, sad, and mad. Unlike girls who have very expansive and expressive feelings, boys can be a bit easier to handle. Help your son understand the emotion; accept that emotion, and move on. Do not go into a 'parent soliloquy' with your son on emotions and rationalizing it. They don't need it and will not appreciate your aim at comfort.

Your response and reaction to the emotions of your son will impact future emotional experiences internally by your son, and how they should be expressed in the future. Therefore you must engage them uniquely but consistently as they are presented. A few key practices are shared from parents and child psychology studies[12].

- Parents need to provide a consistent and transparent environment on good and bad
  » Reinforces our *'Live It don't Tell It'* philosophy (i.e., Hard to punish a kid for lying if they see you lying)
- Accept your child's reaction and emotions, as they are
  » They are real. Telling a kid who is scared, that they aren't is confusing to them (remember—you are their trusted authority on all matters)
- Don't be a stoic—convey your own feelings liberally and literally
  » Helpful to share how your feelings are given your son's actions

---

12   "Helping children regulate emotions - The Incredible Years." http://incredibleyears.com/download/resources-for-parents/helping-children-regulate-emotions.pdf. Accessed 10 Dec. 2016.

- Encourage your child to talk about feelings
- Create open, safe spaces to talk about how they feel without the labeling or judgment of them
  - » An important area is to encourage your child's internal 'self-talk' voice and emotion to be positive and reinforcing. If emotions become buried, self-judgment is possible and ultimately can be quite negative.

An important area is to encourage your child's internal 'self-talk' voice and emotion to be positive and reinforcing. If emotions become buried, self-judgment is possible and ultimately can be quite negative.

An old Cherokee is teaching his grandson about life.

"A fight is going on inside me," he said to the boy.

"It is a terrible fight and it is between two wolves. One is evil – he is anger, envy, sorrow, regret, greed, arrogance, self-pity, guilt, resentment, inferiority, lies, false pride, superiority, and ego." He continued,

*"The other is good – he is joy, peace, love, hope, serenity, humility, kindness, benevolence, empathy, generosity, truth, compassion, and faith.
The same fight is going on inside you—
and inside every other person, too."*

The grandson thought about it for a minute and then asked his grandfather, "Which wolf will win?"

The old Cherokee simply replied, "The one you feed."

CHAPTER 4
CREATING THE BEST MOMENTS FOR GROWTH

TIPS IN THIS CHAPTER:
- ✓ Teach by example
- ✓ Techniques to enrich their minds
- ✓ Instilling responsibility

Feed the passion on day one above all else. The beautiful thing about children is that there are so many day ones! Every new experience, new craft, new book, new school, new class, new game, and new park is a new day one. This means you not only have many opportunities, but you also have a lot of moments where you can be inspirational to your child.

This chapter will explore encouraging this passion and helping you inspire your child in new directions. As the parents, we have the greatest impact on our children by showing them what is important and appropriate in our world, since they arwe likely to mimic our behaviors.

PURSUE PASSION BEFORE PRECISION

PASSION, MECHANICS,
CONSISTENCY, PROFICIENCY

IGNITING THE SPARK

Teach Them by DOING What You Want Them to Do

Teaching by doing in the first few years is the best opportunity for parents and grandparents, as your child is literally mimicking the behaviors he sees to learn how to exist in the world. So be aware of the company your child keeps, both the children and the adults. If your child is constantly around a child who whines, complains, or says "um", she will likely adopt these behaviors. This includes racist, sexist, or other damaging behaviors.

Want fit kids that grow to become healthy adults?
→ You need to physically train your body and eat a nutritious and balanced diet

Want your kid to smoke or do drugs?
→ You should smoke and do drugs

Want your kids to manage failure and loss well?
→ They need your response to be healthy and proactive

This is why some parents obsess over who their children engage with at different ages and how important their surroundings are while growing up. As your child moves from newborn to toddler to grade school, pay extreme attention to the teachers and counselors. Why? Teachers spend an average of 80% of your child's waking hours with them. That is a massive influence. This is why it is so important that your child's teacher is a great person. In cases where your child is not in such a situation, many parents have noted that they have had to move school districts, switched to private schools, or even provide home schooling.

Elon Musk made his own version of home school, and now has his own kids plus a group of kids together to learn applying a more explorative teaching method. In the end, there are options and you have to make the decision on what kind of person you want raising your child.

It is your job to do everything in your power to ensure your child's teachers have all the supplies, resources, and parenting support to do the best job they can. This means respecting him or her, supporting, and allowing the teacher to instruct your child. This means we must teach our children to respect these individuals (coaches too), and keep the responsibility and ownership of the student work with our child. Sadly there was a trend of "helicopter parents" verbally beating up teachers because their kids failed a test—clearly a disconnect in who is the student and responsible.

You must PRACTICE the behaviors and values you cherish. Words are not enough; if you want your child to show respect, you should show respect. If you want your child to play sports, you should play sports. If you do not want your child to smoke, then you should not smoke. More subtle actions: if you do not want your child to be rude, you should not be rude. To teach the rules, you must demonstrate and live the rules.

By living these principles and rules, you are living a life of integrity. Integrity in this case is doing what you know is right whether someone is watching or not watching. It is in these acts that you demonstrate consistently the character your child can adopt and mimic. As you—because we all had them—find activities you choose to change for the betterment for your family, be it smoking, playing video games all night, or weekend golf excursions, you'll have to work consistently to be successful. This lesson will also transfer to your child, which is a bonus. A successful approach is to change how you view these adjustments in your life, by employing the statement "I don't ...." and not "I can't...", and you'll be twice as likely to succeed at your goal. For example, say[13]:

---

13 Patrick, Vanessa M., and Henrik Hagtvedt. "'I Don't' versus 'I Can't': When Empowered Refusal Motivates Goal-Directed Behavior." Journal of Consumer Research, vol. 39, no. 2, 2012, pp. 371–381. www.jstor.org/stable/10.1086/663212.

- **I don't** smoke anymore, and not I can't because of [fill in excuse]
- **I don't** eat fried foods, so I can see my daughter graduate from college
- **I don't** leave town every weekend for golf and miss precious family time

BUILDING PASSION

Our first job is to set a fire of passion for each of these new experiences and to spend less time trying to get it right or perfect. Rules, progression, and refinement can be built. This is important to ensure that they find joy in each new experience to fuel their maturity—this joy becomes a powerful ally in sports, education, and all hobbies.

Here some simple guidelines that you can apply:

1. New experience - make it FUN! (keep it simple and safe)
2. Allow your child 100% control (yes, which is simple and safe) of experience.
3. As repetitions of experience begin to happen, your child will desire to make it less simple and more adult—here is where you begin to improve their mechanics.
4. As they become consistent you can make the experience more and more "adult."
5. Finally he is proficient and you cue them on ways to improve.
6. Repeat for every bit of fun!

**PASSION → MECHANICS →
CONSISTENCY → PROFICIENCY**

Example:	Ice Skating:	Bike Riding:
1. Make it fun	Give her a helmet; water-proof pants & gloves. Skate holding hands or have daughter between legs and brace up under arms.	Bring him to a low risk area—rubber floor playground or small safe parking lot. Give him training wheels, a helmet, a small bike. Use lots of toys and accessories to make it exhilarating.
2. Child 100% control	Skate with your arms just under her arms to catch if falls, but she steers.	Don't yell or shout orders; just encourage and make fun. Set up obstacles to gamify it.
3. Improve movement patterns	As she moves from two-hand holding to one-hand holding; being ready to pick up after she falls—remember she WILL fall. You teach her to keep getting up.	As time goes by you'll likely upgrade his bike to a slightly bigger one and raise training wheels to be less supportive. Keep it challenging now, so he will want to begin increasing the level of difficulty.
4. Mature experience	She is going to want to do turns, spins, and jumps. Encourage and demonstrate progressions.	He will want to start jumping things, going off road, etc. Set up scenarios for it happen (but remember, take baby steps towards the end goal it at first) - have fun!
5. Encourage advances	As they experiment, encourage it, but share an occasional tip to help them succeed at the maneuver being attempted. Here, you are instructing.	

To create the best moments built upon passion, we also need to be mindful of how we act in our daily lives. As parents, we will have the greatest impact on our children by showing them what is important, how we respond to change, and the mental process necessary to learn from new experiences. A strong female role model who has achieved the pinnacle of her sport, twice, shared a great perspective on achieving the best version of her. Such a great lesson—the best version of you.

"I know I'll never [reach] perfection. I can hit excellence. If you strive for perfection, then somewhere along the way, you'll hit the best version of yourself."

Katrin Tanja Davidsdottir, 2x Fittest Woman On Earth[14]

SHOW RESPECT

How cliché is it to say 'show respect'? How often do you mumble remarks like "kids these days!" as you witness a disrespectful act, or hear a comment lacking decency to another human? Both of these situations are missing a key element: respect. It is up to YOU to instill respect and common decency into your child, so that this young generation will not be labeled with such descriptions.

To instill common decency and respect, here are a few key practices that you can adopt into your regular day:

- Respect to your child:
  - » Say please and thank you
- Respect for wait staff:
  - » Speak to them kindly—say please and thank you
  - » Highlight the good they are doing by saying directly to your child, "wow, how thoughtful she was to bring me water when I was coughing"
  - » Speak *of* them kindly. Not only are they doing well, but they are good people, too.
- Respect other people (friends and strangers alike):
  - » Speak to them kindly—say "please" and "thank you"
  - » Do not gossip
  - » Do not complain
  - » Never speak ill of another person, as those you speak with will assume you are/can do the same to them when they are not present too

---

14 "Interview with Katrin Davidsdottir, 2016 CrossFit Games Champion ...." 26 Jul. 2016, http://www.mensfitness.com/life/entertainment/katrin-davidsdottir-interview-2016-crossfit-games-fittest-on-earth. Accessed 13 Dec. 2016.

These consistent practices will transfer nicely into your child. Although the above list only deals with other people we interact with throughout the average day, an equally important group to build respect for is our institutions. These include our military, police, fire departments, religions, the government, and symbols of importance (churches, shrines, holy books, etc...).

We as parents must equally demonstrate and demand respect are had for these and other institutions. We can show disagreement, but it important to educate our children on the importance of these groups. Here are examples of bad habits and their effects:

Parent Behavior:	Child's behavior that mimics adult in future:
Cursing the police when getting pulled over for speeding (in trouble only because you were caught)	May believe goal in life is to behave unsafely, so long as no one catches them (drug use, alcohol abuse, rioting)
Running red lights (while pulling into kid's school)	Breaking the law is OK; disregard for other's safety
Negative remarks about a military action that cause your child to think the military soldiers are bad, and not the mission itself	Lack of appreciation of soldier who died or are injured
Complaining about following the laws	Act with disregard to rules at school, violate work requirements, and social violence
Complaining and faking injuries or reasons to skip jury duty	Replace "jury duty" with school and you can see how this seamlessly transfers to your child's logic in a few years.

I challenge you every day to find other areas where you can find moments where you can demonstrate respect, and thereby improve the future life of your child.

READ

Want your child to be able to read? Want them to be able write? Well, you need to read. Yes, you. The number one way to get your kid to learn to read, be passionate about reading, and gain the benefits of reading (i.e., larger vocabulary; easier progression through English and spelling tests throughout school) is for YOU to read.

Reading progressions to consider	
0-3 years old	Read 1+ book every night for your child (15-20 mins).
3-4 years old	Read 1+ book every night and have her read a word here and there.
4-5 years old	Read every few sentences together. Have fun, make it enjoyable, and be flexible.
5-6 years old	Read every other page of a book together and discuss what was just read. This will develop reading comprehension.
6-7 years old	Read 1 book each and or a chapter ensuring emotions, pauses, and the "voice" is read.
Keep reading!! By now your child should be hungry and desire to finish a book. Typically schools will let them check 1 book out a week too!	

This means you read to your child every night—yes, you get to read to them every night, a blessing. Then, as they begin to become more self-sufficient and you have some leisure time—you read for fun. Trust me, they will notice it. You read, they read, and soon enough, reading becomes a fun. The speed and adoption of this skill varies from child to child. Putting in the effort and making it joyful though will accelerate it. Just as it did for Oprah Winfrey, who was taught to read by her grandmother before the age of three[15].

Reading email/Facebook/news on your phone or tablet does not count. You must read a printed book, just as your child is reading. The practice here will command learning around focused attention. This will aide them in the classroom and in life with larger projects

---

15 Krohn, Katherine E, Oprah Winfrey: Global Media Leader (USA Today) (Krohn, 2002), ISBN 978-1-58013-571-9, p. 9.

> ### A personal experience:
> My daughter as a 2 & 3 year old loved a few specific books that we would read very often. Well, after a while I began to ad-lib a bit of the story, expanding the story to include more detail. I got pretty good and consistent. (You'll see...when you read Barbie becomes a doctor 200x, sometimes variety is necessary.) Well as she became able to read, she started noticing that the words I was reading weren't on the pages. It became a game and shared private moment where we would add to the story long after the page text was done. As of now, my daughter is a voracious reader who puts me to sleep sometimes—my, how times have changed!

LOVE AND WARMTH

Give love and warmth to your child and demonstrate this joyful act with your family members and friends. Love creates a strong bond and helps build the foundation of your child in all things. In fact, according to the longest study of this nature in history, the warmth of childhood relationships between children and their parents had significant impact on their health, professional success, and future relationships.

The Harvard Grant Study began in 1938 and followed 268 students for 75 years. The researchers observed many aspects of the subject's lives, and came away with a striking (perhaps intuitive to parents) takeaways[16]. Love, above all else, was linked to health and long lives. Luckily for us as parents, we can easily give this generously[17].

---

16 "Triumphs of Experience — George E. Vaillant | Harvard University Press." http://www.hup.harvard.edu/catalog.php?isbn=9780674059825. Accessed 16 Dec. 2016.

17 "Grant Study - Wikipedia." https://en.wikipedia.org/wiki/Grant_Study. Accessed 16 Dec. 2016.

Benefits of childhood warmth given by the parents, according to the 75 year study	
Mother's impact:	Earned an average of $87,000 more a year Associated with effectiveness at work
Father's impact:	Lower rates of adult anxiety Greater enjoyment of vacations Increased "life satisfaction" at age 75

How you demonstrate and provide such love is unique and special. Providing this environment is the different than helicopter parenting, where the parents takeaway the ownership and responsibility from the child to engineer a result, and should be given generously. Love was singled out also in the study as a key factor in happiness, and at this young age, parents have the opportunity to demonstrate and give love that'll benefit your child forever[18].

HEALTHY

Food is the energy your child needs, and your child is growing and needs high quality materials to build his/her brain, muscles, and bones. It is our job to start them off right. Care needs to include giving them the nutrients and food they need, when they need them, as well as helping them draw a healthy relationship with food. This is built upon a foundation of you helping them understand where good food comes from and its benefits. A helpful way of thinking about health is to ensure you have all three corners of this triangle.

---

18 "Harvard's 75-Year Study Reveals The Secret To Living A ... - A Plus." 10 Feb. 2015, http://aplus.com/a/75-year-harvard-grant-study-happiness?no_monetization=true. Accessed 16 Dec. 2016.

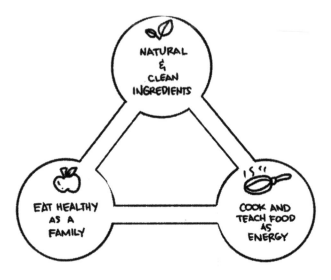

A difficult task for us as parents is selecting food options for our kids that are free from heavy manufactured chemicals, sugar, and mystery ingredients. As the adult, you are the one who has to understand the nutrition ingredient list and see past the marketing language on the packaging. The better you get at buying healthy food, the easier it'll be to allow your child free choice at home. Allowing your child a responsibility and a level of control over their life is a powerful habit.

How do we determine if the food in our hand is healthy[19]?

- Is it in a package?
- Can it survive in your pantry and be viable in a zombie apocalypse?
- Does it have ingredients you don't recognize?
- Is it packed with salt or sugar (i.e., salt and/or sugar is listed as the second or third ingredient in the nutrient list)?
- Did it come with a toy when you bought it?

---

19 "Raising Healthy Eaters - Part I - Dr. Mark Hyman." 20 Nov. 2012, http://drhyman.com/blog/2012/11/20/raising-healthy-eaters-part-i/. Accessed 19 Dec. 2016.

If you answered yes to any of those questions, it is NOT ideal for your child. Certainly trips, treats, parties, and life events must be celebrated without hesitation, but in order for your child to grow up strong and healthy, we must provide the right materials to support their growth. Mark Hyman MD the Medical Director at Cleveland Clinic's Center, encourages such natural food, and is leading the charge in no sugar and higher fat diets - more aligned with his research and widely available in his books.[20]

Example: Even apple sauce isn't simple

In 2016, I went to buy apple sauce. There were two brands available to me:

- Brand 1 was 50 cents cheaper. Ingredients were: apples, high fructose corn syrup, as well as 5 more ingredients.

- Brand 2 ingredients were: apples, plus 1 more ingredient

It is our job as parents to review what is fed to our children. Do not accept marketing, fancy graphics, or anything short of the ingredient list. Apple sauce isn't just apple sauce, just like chicken isn't always chicken at fast food burger chains, etc. Curious? Google "Subway restaurant meat ingredient list," to understand how opaque some restaurant ingredients have become in our age of genetic engineering.

Now the hard part—YOU need to eat what they're eating, too. In order to eat healthily in a way that will properly give our bodies adequate energy and nutrients, we need to *eat meat and vegetables, nuts and seeds, some fruit, little starch and no sugar,* as simply summarized by Greg Glassman, the founder of CrossFit. The more you can have

---

20 "About Dr. Mark Hyman." http://drhyman.com/about-2/about-dr-mark-hyman/. Accessed 19 Dec. 2016.

a lifestyle of healthy living will create the best opportunity for you both have long lives. Personally speaking, you'll also have to reflect on how many sugary drinks and snacks you consume. They are very common in today's food industry.

Finally, we must not give these kids a complex regarding their relationship to food. It is important that we treat food as it is and nothing else. It is not a reward, and you and your kids are not dogs (if you are, you are wicked smart dogs), so let's not create that feedback cycle. This means no rewarding them—or yourself, for that matter—with food after good days, after bad days, or after big accomplishments. Food is for providing energy and energy alone, so keep it simple.

It has been scientifically proven (and personally learned) that if you keep sugar out of your kid's life except for special occasions you will have a more consistently respectful, behaved, polite, child who is a high performer in school and a productive athlete[21]. Medically speaking, reducing sugar intake also reduces the chance of obesity, diabetes, and cavities[22]. Sugar spikes in children's bodies something awful, and it is best we stay away from it.

Note: it is nearly impossible to avoid all sugar, as fruits and juices have it, too. However, is that sugar occurring in a natural form (such as the naturally sweet taste of a banana) or is it chemically processed (such as the unnaturally sweet taste of a lot of fruit juices)? There is a difference between natural and artificial sugars, and these differences cause significant reactions in the human body. One of the most important distinctions is that artificial sugar can make your body crave more sugar. (Have you ever noticed that after you drink a soda, you want something else sugary? This is why.) Pro tip: if it ends in -ose, it's a form of sugar. Don't be fooled!

---

21   "Carbohydrates and Blood Sugar | The Nutrition Source | Harvard T.H. ...." https://www.hsph.harvard.edu/nutritionsource/carbohydrates/carbohydrates-and-blood-sugar/. Accessed 7 Dec. 2016.

22   "Does Sugar Really Make Children Hyper? | Yale Scientific Magazine." 1 Sep. 2010, http://www.yalescientific.org/2010/09/mythbusters-does-sugar-really-make-children-hyper/. Accessed 7 Dec. 2016.

A high fructose corn syrup factory, delicious?[23]

23   "The Murky World of High Fructose Corn Syrup - Mother Linda's." http://
www.motherlindas.com/HFCS_murky.htm. Accessed 6 Dec. 2016.

Techniques to enrich their minds

Kids want to learn—in fact, everything is a learning experience. It is your opportunity to maximize those where you can, and simply be more mindful of situations that can make a long term impression.

The first principle to making these opportunities is the creation of judgment-free zones. This doesn't mean lying, providing false hope, or letting your kid win. Instead, this means allowing for art to be ugly. For coloring to be outside the lines. It means for animals to different colors (purple cows), gravity to not apply, and to make something fly when it is not fully flying. Simply put: precision is the enemy, creative exploration is the intent.

The second principle here is to ignore time. The creation and dabbling of our kids (ideally with us) in these creative exploits is not confined to any single chunk of time. Art, projects, and explorations can stop and restart across an hour, a day, or several weeks. Savor the discovery of new possibilities and allow for your child to make their own path.

To help inspire, a few ideas are broken out below and how they enabled me on this journey. Paint your own path, and feel free to build upon these ideas.

GAMES

Old as time itself, the simplest of games continue to be reinvented in our society (Popular iPhone App "Words with Friends", is really Scrabble, which was Lexiko), and are wonderful vehicles for your child at all ages. The key attributes of good games that will enhance your child's mind are interactive, human-to-human (no electronics), physical (in your hand), featuring clear and simple rules, with obvious winners and losers. These together cut across many different studies that help the development of language, social skills, communication, mathematics, and competition.

A few words of caution: games on a screen, TV, mobile device, and such are shown to being correlated to ADHD[2425]. Gaming on electronics is best kept till above age eight and less than two hours a week.

Card games—awesome and simple for your child. These are easy to enjoy at the youngest of age and fantastic for afternoon one-on-one coffee dates with your little one too. A couple favorites[26]:

Age	Card Game Example	Potential Advantages
1+	Matching games (dinosaurs, ballerinas, vegetables) w/ bright cards	Develops word, sound, object association
3+	"War", and "Uno"	Pattern development; cognitive ability
4+	"31", "21"	Mathematics
8+	Euchre, Poker, Yahtzee	More social adult game which increases child's exposure

Physical games—get hands on with games. Play catch (can be as simple as toss with a favorite stuffed animal or a ball), play kickball, get in the pool, run around, play tag, fly kites, race with cars, make obstacle courses, and corn hole! The goal is games that you can simplify to the child's age to allow for passion to be found in the game, development skill, and progression to more "real" versions as the child reaches that capability[27].

24 "The screens culture: impact on ADHD." 24 Sep. 2011, https://www.ncbi.nlm. nih.gov/pmc/articles/PMC3220824/. Accessed 6 Dec. 2016.

25 "Screen Fixation and A.D.H.D. - The New York Times." 9 May. 2011, http:// www.nytimes.com/2011/05/10/health/views/10klass.html. Accessed 6 Dec. 2016.

26 "Cognitive Development Domain - Child Development (CA Dept of ...." http:// www.cde.ca.gov/sp/cd/re/itf09cogdev.asp. Accessed 7 Dec. 2016.

27 "The cognitive benefits of play: Effects on the learning brain." http://www. parentingscience.com/benefits-of-play.html. Accessed 7 Dec. 2016.

BOOKS & SUPPLIES

Mail, who doesn't love receiving mail? Well, I think everybody actually only likes receiving cards and packages. The excitement of opening a package or letter is strong for everyone. In our age of online ordering where we probably receive more packages than actual cards, we have a great opportunity to engage our children.

Think of all of orders you place online. Now, what if you added one item for your child? These aren't gifts, but fun books, crafts, or something to be used in active play. When I looked at my embarrassingly serious list of Amazon orders from last year I had 55 orders, and I included a $2-7 item for my daughter in roughly half of them. Now some of these were purely educational—lots of books, but some were glue, glitter, others were sporty items.

Another bonus to these online orders: BOXES. Let me just say, if you are on your first child and haven't passed age two yet, you are in for some fun. Boxes are SUPER fun. Kids make forts, bird houses, luggage, and more things out of boxes. Frankly I had a hard time getting rid of boxes for a while.

A final treat of ordering together is a shared foundation of companionship and experience with your child each time you open these packages. Shopping doesn't have to be mindless, and definitely not materialistic. Be creative!

CREATIVE SPACES

Make a desk, a corner, a room, a table, or anything that is permanent and designate it for creative work for your child. You should make it impervious to harming your floors, your walls, and frankly anything else. The idea is you should feel 100% fine with a three year old painting a piece of paper with bright paint in this space without grabbing the brush in fear of something being ruined. Prep a space and teach that it is for art. You'll save a thousand grey hairs.

Setup your creative space with plenty of markers, paper, glue sticks, safe scissors, stickers, and a couple craft kits from target or Michaels. This may sound ornate, but the total cost is probably $20. Then let them at it. Over time, things will come in favor and out of favor. You'll put things on the wall, take things down, and the room will transform in the rich colors they choose to use.

Have fun!

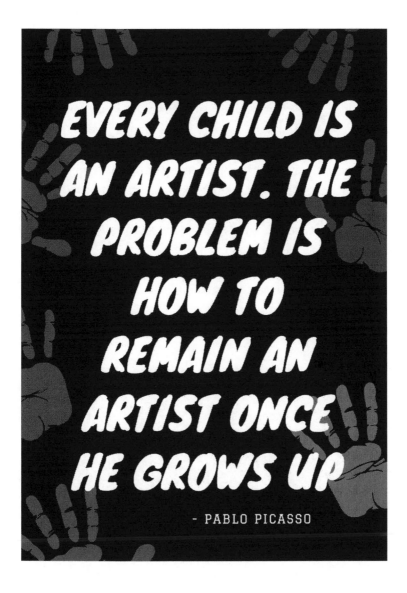

TEAMWORK

There is a strong need for us as parents to instill and allow naturally the ability for our sons and daughters to self-manage. A theme of structuring their learning environment to allow independent play and the responsibility to solve their own problems is strong among exceptional parents. This leads to great teamwork and is reflected in our child's ability to engage positively in team sports and the classroom.

We must encourage and treat equally both the girls and the boys in this area. As a parent we must step in when we must, but only once the actions of one or the group creates consequences that mandate it. Beyond those moments the more we can encourage kids to self-manage and solve their squabbles the better.

This doesn't mean we permit bullying or harm, but just the opposite: we teach our child that teamwork and group play require respect for all kids. These teachings should be balanced with the advice of parents shared throughout this book, but at a minimum include the following:

- Advocating for yourself against bullies
- Choosing good friends
- Creative safe play areas

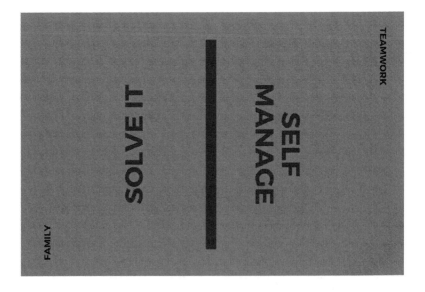

Instilling responsibility

This is more a concept for the parents (in fact the #1 attribute desired by all parents for their children), but one that will pay dividends in the long term[28]. The concept here is you as the parent are trying to create pride in accomplishing a task, and the ability to complete a task from start to finish. Let's break these down first.

Pride in accomplishing a task—"pride" meaning we want our child to not be defined by it but to own that which they did. "Accomplishing" is specifically stated as not "win," "succeed," or any such judgmental term. We are simply seeking that awareness that they DID it. Finally "a task." This isn't work but instead this is an activity. We as adults create checklists, work calendars, and are a bit too wound up on this idea of completing work. There is joy in accomplishing a task in and of itself. We must aim to create that atmosphere.

Dr Ginott and Dr. Rotella both highlight several perspectives here and I encourage you to dive into their published work[29][30]. We as parents want to set up situations that allow our child to develop an association with their effort to the feeling of accomplishment and pride. Here are a few points of performance:

- Focus on the effort and not the result when praising/discussing
- If a failure occurred, identify what was a glimmer of good or hope for future
- Help your child develop a path to reaching goal (no matter the size)

---

28 "Families may differ, but they share common values on parenting." http://www.pewresearch.org/fact-tank/2014/09/18/families-may-differ-but-they-share-common-values-on-parenting/. Accessed 19 Dec. 2016.

29 "Between Parent and Child." http://www.betweenparentandchild.com/. Accessed 7 Dec. 2016.

30 "How Champions Think by Bob Rotella | Official ...." http://www.simonandschuster.com/books/How-Champions-Think/Bob-Rotella/9781442376298. Accessed 7 Dec. 2016.

- State how the result of their work benefited others, you, family, etc.
- Allow your child to infer positive feelings and sense of ownership
- Pause, listen, and use silence to allow your child to explore his/her feelings

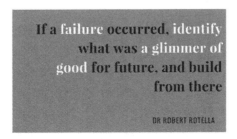

If a failure occurred, identify what was a glimmer of good for future, and build from there

DR ROBERT ROTELLA

JOBS

Give your child a job, as early as possible, and continue to increase their jobs/chores as they grow in age. As simple as it seems, it is a powerful action. First, think of the moment you were given the responsibility for something big at work. That feeling of trust, that sense of anxiety around the murkiness of succeeding, and the anticipated response from your teammates upon successful completion. In addition to this empowering feeling, chores (along with love) are directly tied to later success in life according to the longitudinal "Harvard Grant Study"[31].

THAT is what you are creating for your child when you give them jobs. Jobs can be simple, but the key traits are the following:

- Safe
- Can be done independently
- Low to zero permanent harm possible (to your home, possessions or them!)
- ZERO yelling, criticizing, or judging if anything goes awry
- Only 1-2 "tips" when the child is doing the task

---

31 "'How to Raise an Adult" Julie Lythcott-Haims. Henry Holt & Company, 2015, Print.

Jobs are best something that is not a chore or errand, but a duty. Something that can be done or not done. Jobs can also be something you initially did as the parent, but we need to be careful in these handoffs. Good examples of jobs:

Having your child make their own lunch (starting at age five) with guidance and good options

- "Packing" her toys/coloring book for a trip
- Organizing their creative/toy rooms
- Organize their clothes drawers
- Walking dog

Jobs may begin for your child as early as four, such as simply clearing their own dishes. Additional jobs can and should be added to their list for as they age. One great family shared how they post all of the jobs that need to be done and by when. The three kids in the house then decide between themselves who gets what job and by when. There is no parent intervention to make it fair, but there are quality standards expected. These jobs also, in this example, are not paid but instead 'cost of living'. There are additional bigger jobs that any child can elect to do for cash, such as vacuuming the whole two story house for $6.

Whether it is a job, chore, activity, or pursuit (such as karate) one concept that was emphasized in the upbringing of luminaries, such as Elon Musk, is the concept of seeing things through. If the child commits to a course, they must see it through to the end. Now near term goals can be established by using the principle, as Maye Musk put it, "...if you start something, you finish it.[32]"

---

32   "How Elon Musk's Mom (and her Twin Sister) Raised the First Family of ...."
21 Oct. 2015, http://www.vanityfair.com/news/2015/10/elon-musk-family-maye-musk. Accessed 12 Dec. 2016.

GAMES—LOSING AND WINNING

While games were highlighted earlier, they bear repeating here. Specifically, when games are played, we need to teach being a gracious loser and humble winner. This doesn't mean we don't express our disappointment or joy based on the outcome. Simply we make sure we express this in a respectful way, as how you win—so shall your child.

A habit of some parents is to allow their kid to win. Don't. Play the games honestly and fairly. If you win, you win. Some games are just too complex for your child and should be held off until they are older. If we don't take mind to their maturity it is possible they will forever hate the game where they always lost.

Encourage them to enjoy their win. Give them a high five. Smile. Say congratulations. Make it a big deal. If they lose, ask for your high five. This reciprocation lays the groundwork for a long life of good sportsmanship and sets the stage for them building coping skills in the face of adversity. As in games and in pursuits of passion, the quality of hardiness, as studied by psychologists, Suzanne Kobasa and Salvatore Maddi of University of Chicago are built upon the three C's—Commitment, Control, and Challenge.

The ability to overcome childhood adversity is related to a personality structure called 'hardiness.' It's your hardiness that 'allows you to deal with the stress of solving personal or work problems' and 'the hardy person is able to stay positive under difficult circumstances.

—Suzanne Kobasa

PARENTING MOMENTS

There will be moments when times are hard. Your child will go nuclear and all the emotion possible of being expressed will be unleashed. These honestly happened occasionally for me, and they just are what they are: OPPORTUNITIES!

I had a few early parenting moments during our games (chutes and ladders I believe) where she didn't follow a rule, I said she had to follow the rule, and she blew up. Well, after that I put the game up and three weeks later we finally played it again, fairly this time. The actions you take in these moments will define whether you will have twenty more on the same topic, or one. Bottom line: if you teach in these parenting moments you'll both be happier.

Planned parenting moments: sometimes you see behavior that is unacceptable. Maybe your child is being selfish, hitting someone, etc. Unfortunately, if you do not nip these in the bud they will fester to be something very difficult to manage. In those cases, you can consider creating a situation (safely) where this behavior happens, and then you parent. This will suck, I promise, for at least twenty minutes. Once it is over though, you will see rewards.

As a parent you have to parent. Don't apologize for behavior—correct it, teach. Ensure your child knows that your role is the parent, and that this responsibility bears consequences that your child will pay in the future.

> *Today we are Parents;*
> *when your child*
> *is an adult,*
> *you can be friends*

WHAT YOU THINK YOU BECOME

WHAT YOU FEEL YOU ATTRACT

WHAT YOU IMAGINE YOU CREATE

- BUDDHA

CHAPTER 5
CREATING THE BRIGHTEST FUTURE

IDEAS IN THIS CHAPTER:
- ✓ Communicating
- ✓ Creating a life of experiences

What can you possibly do to help set up your child for the brightest future? Well, this chapter is full of habits, activities, and tricks that you can apply. The ways of thinking and habits here are drawn from luminaries in the early childhood development field, current research, and examples drawn from parents from around the world. This is structured in a manner to give you concrete ideas from the parent's perspective. If you are interested in the science and philosophy, please visit the long list of sources and references listed in the back of this book and online.

Communicating

SPEAK AS AN ADULT
Seems simple, but it means you speak to your child patiently, completely, and with respect. Dr. Haim Ginott, who was a clinical psychologist, child therapist, and parent educator, as well as author of Between Parent and Child, emphasizes that the language that we use should be protective of feelings, not critical of behaviors. In a simple explanation, we as parents must speak children as they are guests in our home.

CONCISELY
"What is air?"

"Why does Gabriel have two dads/moms?

Your child does not want a "parent answer," but instead a crisp answer to questions in ten seconds or less.

You need to be concise, and if your child expands the question, then you can expand the answer. Adults are too wordy, we try to be too complete, and miss what is really being asked by the child.

In most cases the child is looking for comfort, understanding, and a nod from you to clarify a conflict they are or have observed. Your child is not looking for a political debate or a sermon on political correctness. In the other cases, your child is observing life and curious. We want to encourage and never quell their curiosity, so remember - "because" is never a real answer but instead is an opportunity to help you both discover the answer.

The most important thing is to not stop questioning
- Albert Einstein

ABSOLUTES
Building on the "concisely" comments above, you also need to pick

a side. Meaning if you are asked if you love something, the answer needs to be yes or no. Favorite color? Pick one color.

Don't dance around the issue, question, or topic. Be confident and they will be confident. Have an opinion and they will have an opinion. Respect that you each have different opinions, and that respect will transfer to others. This will transfer as your child grows up and is given the opportunity to share their ideas and opinion.

EMBRACE YOUR CHILD'S VIEW

Your child perceives the world differently every day. Each new day they see, hear, and learn new "truths" about the world. As they gain more experiences, their emotions and feelings are put in conflict with what they hear and see in the world. An example that makes me sad comes from my own daughter:

A personal expample

As a young child (age 4-6) she was taught that "if you see trash, pick it up." She and I stopped every time to pick up trash everywhere we went, and at some point she realized that people (other adults) were putting the trash there. She learned that not everyone stopped to pick it up. This conflict troubled her and it saddened me; the world (and I) failed our children in this lesson of care and protection of our world. She and I then spoke deeply about 'bad people,' and together we had to come to terms on these conflicts she was feeling.

Ultimately, we must not deny their feelings, dispute their perceptions, or challenge their opinions. We as parents must acknowledge them, as advised by Dr. Ginott. Only then can we help them navigate their emotions, and allow our child to feel respected and accepted as a person who belongs.

NEVER SAY, "BE SAFE"

What does that communicate?

How does your child apply that to their action?

We, as parents, have had decades of learnings and experience. We have made and felt the bad decisions, and so when we see our child climbing we think of the thousand and one ways it could go a foul, and we say "be safe." Consider that your child doesn't have that experience, and flashing a warning doesn't help.

Instead, let's communicate information on HOW to be careful and avoid the mistake you are envisioning. First, don't shout caution and worry upon your child, but instead highlight how to proceed with care and skill. If she is running, help her by calling out to keep her legs high and eyes forward. If he is climbing, instruct as if he were climbing a ladder—"hand, hand, foot, foot..."—so long as a hand and a foot are solidly in place he'll never fall. When you deal out these details you are being their parent and giving instruction that they can forever apply and build upon.

Guidance is the truly valuable lesson and helpful words that our child needs. Stating the problem and possible solutions is helpful. More helpful would be exploring the process of identifying solutions, thus helping your child to learn to discover independently.

> *GIVE GUIDANCE - NOT FEAR*
> *PROCESS & EXPERIMENTATION*
> *ALLOW FAILURE AND LESSONS*

While we as parents can teach our children about the world, some skills and abilities must be learned independently. This requires allowing failures, mistakes, and freedom for your child. Julie Lythcott-Haims, author of "How to Raise Successful Kids—Without Over-Parenting" goes even further and presses the criticality of giving children independence, free of parenting manipulation (of outcomes). In her TED Talk, Lythcott-Haims shares that to do the opposite robs our child of self-efficacy—a most selfish act of parents that creates long-term difficulties. She goes further to emphasize that by our "over help, overprotection and over direction and hand-holding, we deprive our kids of the chance to build self-efficacy, which is a really fundamental tenet of the human psyche, far more important than that self-esteem they get every time we applaud.[33]"

NEVER CHANGE A POSITION

Child: Can I jump off the couch?
Parent: No!
(30 seconds later)
Parent: Well, yes if...
(How seriously will your child now consider your statements?)

Either something is safe or it is not. It is either allowed or it isn't. When conditions and exceptions are added, it challenges your authority and state of guardianship with your child. Children will constantly seek out the finest edge of what is allowed. Therefore it is more important that you have clear lines and not grey lines open to interpretation. It'll save you in the long term.

PRAISE EFFORT

Here is an area deep in research but something parents and business leaders often fail at in the beginning. When a child does anything you feel is praise worthy, focus on the specific acts. Meaning, state what has been improved, how something looks, the impact of it, and/or how it makes you (the parent) better/feel. The key is to not speak to character traits, or say things like "you did a good job".

---

33 "Julie Lythcott-Haims: How to raise successful kids—without ... - TED.com." https://www.ted.com/talks/julie_lythcott_haims_how_to_raise_successful_kids_without_over_parenting/transcript. Accessed 16 Dec. 2016.

Dr. Carol Dweck highlights this in her research, too. She highlights how having a fixed mindset vs. open mindset at the earliest age, and how we are praised directly impacts our lives long term. In fact, according to her work, we all start at the same point in early childhood, but a gap widens every year as a result of these fixed mindsets. Our job is to encourage and praise the effort, the process, and allow our children to discover the value in failing (and getting back up).

Demonstrative Examples

When your child has done something praiseworthy and a good job:

- State the WHY they did a good job
  - Identify what they did well
  - This reinforces the positive feelings

- Don't say "you are so smart"
  - This is a judgment on character and must be avoided

- Say what you want your child to do (positive instruction) and not "don't"
  - Say "Walk" vs. "Don't run"

FAIL OFTEN

The ability for children to fearlessly try new things is critical in their growing and finding love and passion. Failing is a powerful learning experience and one that we must teach. We must teach that when they fail, they evaluate what can be done differently, and try again. Never should we critique a personal trait or character ("You have no balance! That is why you can't ride a bike," or "you are not strong enough.").

The process of discovery, finding a positive in a failure, and building a belief that with hard work he is capable of anything is our top priority as parents. Through this our child can learn and become proficient in anything to their natural maximum capability!

A common thread among the luminaries highlighted throughout this book was that they grew up without fear of scorn or harm for their unconventional elementary school startup efforts. "Even if [these kids] had to fix the mess or apologize for breaking something or screwing up, they were never punished for it," shares Margot Machol Bisnow in her book *Raising an Entrepreneur: 10 Rules for Nurturing Risk Takers, Problem Solvers and Change Makers.*

AVOID NEGATIVE LOGIC

"After your bath, it is bed time."

"As soon as we get home, you are doing your homework."

These seem safe, but they are negative logic. Meaning that the next activity is unpleasant/boring/a chore/not nearly as fun as the present moment. The problem is you'll be fighting uphill every moment up to the bath, during the bath, and after the bath.

Instead, time constrain the activity, so that way it is inevitable. You can restate the above by saying, "if we have time after your bath we'll read stories," or "the sooner we get home and get your homework done, the sooner we can..." This is simply putting a positive after the activity and constraining the possibility of doing it by time—yes, you'll have to demonstrate your constitution at one point and that'll not be a fun night.

OPTIMISM

We can choose to believe in ourselves and thus to strive, to risk, to persevere, and to achieve. Or we can... rationalize our failures, inventing excuses for our mediocrity.

Simon & Schuster

Optimism and achieving a mental confidence about how you approach life is a powerful contributor to success across all facets of life. We as parents must bring forth optimism in all situations and train our children to bring this powerful mental strength into their life. Challenge yourself on how you view success and disappointments. It is vital for you to cherish and celebrate the good and move on from the mistakes, or else those mistakes will be imprinted on subconscious.

Mentally strengthening yourself is a capability that'll reward you in life, professionally and personally. Carrying this forward into your child's early development will return compound benefits at a much earlier age. A great book quoted above, How Champions Think by sports psychologist Dr. Bob Rotella, drives forward concepts that very applicable. One tip and challenge I have transferred to my own parenting was the following:

When your child brings home homework, focus on the CORRECT answers and not the WRONG answers. Orient their mind to recall what they did correct to receive the high score. Help them re-visualize the hard work. Don't bury their subconscious on "why did you miss these?" Be clear and supportive of hard work and doing well, but navigate the balance and build that optimism muscle.

> The ones who are crazy enough to think they can change the world, are the ones who do.
>
> STEVE JOBS

Creating a life of experiences

We really don't know what our child will love, pursue passionately in life, or create for the world. The only thing we can do is expose them to a broad array of experiences. This exposure should be done though with intention on two points.

The first is to set them up on a pursuit of proficiency in a given discipline. This doesn't mean expert level or a heavy commitment of time, but simply ensuring they are capable in these areas. (We'll talk about each briefly below.)

The second is allowing for the teachings of these experiences to take hold with our child. Each of the below areas expose natural lessons: social skills, ability to focus the mind, empathy for others, and more. You have the hard job of not protecting your child from these lessons as they happen.

How your child develops and matures is not fixed, so constantly seek out such opportunities. In fact, YOU are still in this category. By personally seeking proficiency and new lessons, you will grow too, and be a stunning role model for your child.

MUSIC WE SHARE

What you play around your child matters. It is important to pay careful attention to the variety, the mood, the aggressiveness, the words, and the artists themselves. Of course, you want to play music you will tolerate and eventually love (as you familiarize them to your music preferences), but for the first eight years be considerate of the following to reward your child with maximum exposure:

- **Variety** - Jazz, blues, pop, kids, a cappella, instrumental, rock, electronic, and show tunes
- **Mood** - Slow, scary, happy, bright
- **Aggressiveness** - shouting/screaming singers
- **Words** - your child will memorize every word of the music you play for them

- **Artists** - seek out a balance of male & female singers, and multi-races to expose your child to a variety of dialects

MUSIC WE MAKE

Drums, horns, microphones, and any box that is lying around tend to be childhood favorites for making music. Kids love the making of sounds and then forming these into music. The joys of you hearing your child recognize sound and then to combine these into melodies is amazing. It can also be a bit painful, but it gets better... louder, yes, but better too.

At about the age of six or seven, music lessons are a good idea if your means allow for them. Nothing intense, but a day a week will help develop a basic awareness to music structure and how to read music. This will also transfer to keeping a beat when they dance, play sports, and similar pursuits.

On a budget, you can easily grab a kid sized piano for $20 and print for free music from online. You don't need a grand piano to introduce your child to music.

SCIENCE

Exploring our world is fun and amazing—here is your chance (for boys and girls) to make it real life. This is why kids are always playing in the dirt with rocks and sticks—there is an amazing world right below their feet! The best you can do is to ignite their passion; show them how interesting this world can be, and get hands on!

PLAY IN NATURE—IN THE DIRT AND WITH BUGS

Lift a rock, explore what you see. Go on a short "hike" into nature and get off the beaten trail. SHOW your child how to explore. EXPLAIN the fun details about the tree that beetle, the worm, and each interesting bit.

Ignite their passion and help them understand how nature works.

ROCKETS, DRONES, AND FLYING

We live in such a cool time where it is very easy for you to gain access to these technologies to teach your child about flight. Even better, you don't have to own any of these—you can simply find live demonstrations, watch YouTube videos, or make paper models by hand with them.

Here are some ideas to get you started (personal note, my daughter loves this category, so don't be shy about it with your little lady):

- **Rockets** - YouTube videos of Elon Musk rockets. Then jumping to images about the space station and eventually in evenings looking at stars. *(Schools typically start teaching about the planets around the age of four.)*
- **Drones** - Find someone flying it, and get close. These are great to show a child given they are pretty quiet. Plus, the video screen on the controls makes it easy to watch.
- **Flying** - Paper airplanes, air shows, balloons, and pretty much anything your child can do to be weightless is always a blast (jumpy castles, trampolines). Have fun—you too!

GROW STUFF!

Origination of life is amazing, and one you are currently preciously raising. Sharing this with your child is possible by growing little plants in your house. A few simple ideas to explore are below. Please note "simple" is our goal here—we want something that is low maintenance, small space, and nearly guaranteed to work.

- Veggies
  - » A bit higher maintenance and best in the kitchen
  - » Bean sprouts
  - » Potatoes
- Mini-plants in your house
  - » Plant 3-6 at a time (typically at Home Depot for $3)
  - » Place in child's window

MAKE THINGS

How do you make a building? What are the parts of a fort? These are just a few of the questions you answer by making things. The best way to explore the world of machines and building is to first assemble and disassemble them!

In the beginning you'll be making very basic objects—binoculars, buildings, airplanes, trains, hats, etc.—but as ambitions and skills increase, so shall what is created and what they understand. That is how our active play here will feed and contribute to their lifelong enjoyment.

- (Simple) Binoculars—old paper towel/tissue paper tube rolls, taped together, and even more creative by adding decorations
- Buildings—wood blocks, Legos, Jenga blocks, old Amazon cardboard boxes are all perfect. Even more fun if you add a few characters (Legos, figurines)
- Airplanes—Paper airplanes using any type of paper, http://www.amazingpaperairplanes.com/Simple.html and of course you can get the bigger foam versions.

PROGRAMMING

While this really belongs in "make things," I have separated it here to draw extra emphasis on it. Our world will be heavily leaning towards technology for both pleasure and for most career tracks. So, the more we ensure our child has a depth of understanding of these computers and gadgets, the better!

Our goal with programming is to expose the power of controlling these electronic systems. We want to find the easiest ways of arming our child to view programming like using pencils to sketch drawings. If we can achieve that, the computer languages and programming methods can come later on, fueled by our child's curiosity.

Beyond the basic coding and general proficiency, we are also looking to expand their minds on how these electronics come together and work. Allowing your kid to mentally leap and understand the breakdown of these devices will remove any fears of them using them in the future—a powerful characteristic. Here are some programming systems (message me online for updated details) that are powerful and simple:

- Apple's mobile device kid lab - Swift Playgrounds
- Visual kids programming, Scratch from MIT

Finally, learn to view programming in the same way that you would view building with Legos or Lincoln Logs—your child is building something, only this time with electronic pieces. This advice is especially pertinent if you are not computer savvy. Computer technology is not going anywhere, and even though your generation might be unfamiliar with the ins and outs of programming, your child's peers won't be. In this scenario, we wholeheartedly recommend the earlier principle of "learn it with them." What a fantastic opportunity to expand your knowledge of the world—and this one might impress your friends even more than your nail painting ability!

BE THEIR OWN ADVOCATE

As part of parenting, we have to allow our children to develop independence. If anything was taught by the last generation, it was that "helicopter parenting or the act of over parenting children to the point where they lack their own independence or ability to function without oversight, creates a weaker independent spirit in children when compared to prior generations. You have an opportunity to allow your child to be their own advocate throughout their young age. The most obvious opportunities for this tend to be in classroom, sports, and when dealing with bullies.

"Being their own advocate" means they speak up to a teacher, adult, coach, or bully, and speak their mind. This is done with confidence, strength, and when it is the right thing to do. This also applies to them doing their own tasks—chores, homework, special project, and extracurricular. This applies equally to girls and boys, as life skill this is very valuable. How they articulate and face these moments is unique to the scenario, and some real life examples are included to guide you.

Advocating Opportunity	Parenting Move
Child doesn't like their placement on sports	Child must approach the coach directly and state feelings, and ask what they need to do to progress
Child says coach makes them do all these annoying practices	Instruct child to approach coach and ask/seek out to understand what these practices will lead into, i.e., what is the intention (get to run fast; somersaults, etc...)
Bully in neighborhood	Child must tell bully to stop or not play together. Parent role is to ensure safety but impossible to intervene

EMPATHY

Being thoughtful for others around you
Caring and coming to the aide of those in need
Connecting authentically

Imagine your child helping a school kid who dropped their books, or defending them from a bully. See your child into the future and visualize them coming to the aid of someone who is hurt. These are powerful images that probably bring a smile to your face, as they should. In these imagined scenarios, your child is helping bring warmth and goodness to the world.

Now think of those same scenarios, but your kid is the one who is being defended from a bully or being helped home after twisting her ankle. These bring a bit of an anxious feeling I imagine, as now you recognize, as I did, how critical teaching empathy is in our society.

Teaching empathy, as much as it is possible, relies mostly on you and I as parents. Some children are very empathetic naturally. For those who are not, the best we can do is teach duty and the importance of coming to another's aid. Here are some examples that you can leverage in your favor:

Parent instructive moments:

- Being the leader in helping someone who has been injured (albeit random, but your actions are so important when the chance arises)
- Volunteer at homeless/distressed person shelter or activities
- Participate in can drives, making homeless packages, gifts for saved domestic violence homes
- Write letters to deployed troops
- Visit other sick children in the hospital. This is obviously an incredibly mature thing to do, and should only be done if your child is ready. However, what a kind and powerful thing to do for other children!

ATHLETIC

Physically move together with your child! The direct hands-on experiences will last a long time and build confidence in their self. Bonus is you get to experience life with them and not simply be an observer.

Seek out athletic activities that are great solo and as team sports. My favorites are catch, gymnastics, ice skating/roller skating, and kickball. Yours can be anything, just do it with them and seek out their friends to do it, too. Help your child build a base of experiences with others to grow and strengthen their friendships. Suggestions for fun together:

- **Catch**—Tennis balls are great for young age indoors. In addition to catch itself, you can play by rolling and light tosses. Using balloons in volleyball is great, too. Basically grab anything that won't shatter the TV and make a game of it.
- **Gymnastics**—Headstands, cartwheels, handstands, flips on bars, forward rolls, front flips, and back flips are all fun and reasonable to learn for your child and you! All you need is a space about 10ft

wide. Adding a thick mat will help soften any falls, and is easy to stow away too. I like the 2 inch thick mats, and have found the "We Sell Mats" brand on Amazon to have good products.

- **Ice skating/roller skating**—Get in the cold and get gliding! You can do this year round and I definitely recommend doing it once a month or every two months. I recommend the following:
  - » a helmet - if hockey players wear them, your kid should too (at least for a year or two)
  - » waterproof gloves
  - » thick and long socks to fit skates up to calf
  - » layers up top
- **Kickball**—Less skill required than baseball and tennis, but still a team sport and easy to do at a moment's notice.

Beware the scheduling and busy excitement that comes with loading up your child with activities. New parents can become obsessed with signing their child up for varied activities across the week and on weekends. Depending on where you live, your circle of friends may cause you to enroll your four, six, or nine year old up for too many activities. This is generally the result of desiring to give your child an edge by being proficient in a multi-disciplinary of sports—baseball, karate, gymnastics, piano, math lessons (at age five!), flag football, and more. This overburden actually can harm your child, exhaust you mentally, harm their educational development at a young age, and stretch your finances.Great parents highlighted their preference for one to two activities per week, maximum, including weekends. The activity should be something your child desires to try and is set up in a manner that fits their ability. Ideally you'll be able to combine an artist activity and a physical activity, but each child's passions are different.

Case Example: Lose intensity of scheduling your child

Several parents highlighted they had to ban certain sports, despite neighborhood friends' involvement.

A few neighborhood baseball groups in Georgia for five year olds require two practices a week and had two games a week. These practices started at 7:30pm—which is a common bedtime.

This was a tough choice for the parents, as the matching of activities is a common trick to allow for adult social time while kids are participating. You have to decide what is right and what isn't feasible. An exhausted child and family is a recipe for disaster and difficulty.

IF YOU DECIDE TO DO
SOMETHING
YOU NEED TO DO IT
SERIOUSLY
BECAUSE OTHERS ARE
PUTTING IN
THEIR TIME
HAVE FUN AND HAVE
RESPECT
FOR THOSE LEADING IT

Dr. Kaywork to her children

CHAPTER 6
AVOIDING THE BIGGEST REGRETS AND MISTAKES

CAUTIONS AND LESSONS IN THIS CHAPTER:
- ✓ No crybabies
- ✓ Avoid raising a potato head
- ✓ Saving your house from destruction
- ✓ Bargaining the present for the future

An important point raised in the beginning, but which bears repeating, is that you as the parent are the ultimate arbiter of what is right and wrong for your child. There are not books, studies, doctors, and others who can tell you exactly how to handle every situation. Instead, we can only provide approaches on what has worked, and hopefully by sharing these insights you can benefit from our successes and painful lessons.

This chapter highlights those moments where hindsight is 20:20, and how with a bit of adjustment a child's life may go on a different course.

No crybabies

A hot-button issue today that has arisen across the globe is the lack of independence, maturity, seriousness, and inability to lose found in children today. This appears to be solely the effect of how parents raised these children. This is good, as it means you can do better.

This doesn't require you to send your kid to boot camps or to be severe, but as we've shared previously, there are a few situations you can leverage in your favor.

WINNING ISN'T NORMAL

This is a hard concept but it is vital to raising your child. You must teach that winning isn't normal, but worth every bit of effort to strive for and something to celebrate those who achieve these milestones.

Winning Isn't Normal, a renowned book by sports psychologist Keith Bell, gets to the heart of this idea. We absolutely must instill the notion that we and our children must put in the work necessary to succeed. At the same time, we must make it clear that it is a challenge to achieve greatness. Ultimately, there is a balance that must be struck between putting in hard work and performing to the best of our ability, and it is imperative that we teach our children the relationship between these two actions. Here is a powerful message I took away from Keith and have applied in my own life:

Winning is unusual. And as such, it requires unusual action. In order to win, you must do extraordinary things. You can't just be one of the crowd. The crowd doesn't win. You have to be willing to stand out and act differently."

Keith Bell

SITUATIONS WHERE YOU CAN REINFORCE/AVOID:

- **Everyone gets a trophy**—best to avoid these encounters and seek out situations where skill and hard work are rewarded, but not always possible. Afterwards, you as the parent can speak on who won and who didn't, and what is needed to be the winner.
- **Share when you fail**—often as parents we don't speak when we missed a promotion, were fired, didn't get our lease after four tries, and other "adult" activities. Sanitize the details and share it with your child. They should enjoy when you succeed and don't.
- **Classroom politics**—There will be plenty of times where your child isn't voted to be the classroom leader or the team captain, and must follow that leader. Teaching your kid how to mentally and socially behave will make them a valuable team member when they are in both roles.

IT'S NOT ALWAYS ABOUT YOU

It is not all about your little one. You must allow your child to be capable of entertaining themselves, solving problems with others, and sorting out situations. The biggest crime you can commit is making every waking moment about your child.

Birthdays are the best reinforcement—every child's birthday forces every other child to experience that it isn't about them. Someday it will be their day, but more often than not in a single year, it isn't. Set them up to appreciate these moments celebrating these birthdays, but please avoid those monster gift bags for all of the attendees, as they ruin the lesson!

How you respond to your child plays a big role in their view of priority in the world. If you interrupt phone calls, work, adult conversations, other kids, or simply cease what you are doing to cater to your child… well, that is going to lead to a very tiring life, for everyone. It'll also lead to acute experiences later in life where the world isn't at their beck and call.

Case Example: Lesson on role reversals for a big brother

An active family with two boys discovered a fantastic and tough lesson.

As each boy was a couple years apart, the youngest had no choice but to be "dragged" around to the oldest one's activities and watch the oldest practice or compete. That was true until the youngest became old enough to have their own activities that required the older brother to become the spectator. Suddenly it wasn't always the oldest son show, but also the youngest.

The roles reversed for the oldest from being a player to a spectator, and it was reinforced with countless conversations between the parent and the oldest on why it is so important for him to go to his younger brother's activities. The oldest was used to all of his family coming to watch him, but when he had to begin reciprocating, it was a tough lesson.

As the example above highlights, your family will grow and that will create opportunity to teach these lessons. This great family seized upon it, and instead of splitting the parents to attend each game or creating a scheduling circus, they simply reversed the roles. This is similar to another story where I heard the parents joined karate with the kids, and while the parents train, the kids watch, and then the next hour they switch from training to spectating.

Avoid raising a potato head

LIMIT TELEVISION

Sadly, kids don't learn from watching TV. Televisions make terrible babysitters, and given the immensity of advertisements, little value is to be drawn from kids watching these daily. There is hard science that proves kids do not learn language from DVD or online televisions. The science also proves kids are more likely to form ADHD and other cognitive abilities when they are given too much "screen time." The addictive effect of TV (and all screens) results in part from the release of dopamine, and is why Dr. Peter Whybrow, director of neuroscience at UCLA, calls screens "electronic cocaine" and Chinese researchers call them "digital heroin." In fact, Dr. Andrew Doan, the head of addiction research for the Pentagon and the US Navy—who has been researching video game addiction—calls video games and screen technologies "digital pharmakeia" (Greek for drug)[34].

TV watching households consume about 14 hours of television a week, and this doesn't include any long form shows such as movies or sports events[35]. That is essentially an entire waking day of the week lost to TV, and works out to roughly four hours of commercials a week[36].

There is a time for TV and making these moments family time, or a short bit of private time for a young child in a house full of older kids. These situations can be beneficial, sure. When watching TV, engage with your family during the show to create an interactive environment,

34 "It's 'digital heroin': How screens turn kids into psychotic junkies | New ...." 27 Aug. 2016, http://nypost.com/2016/08/27/its-digital-heroin-how-screens-turn-kids-into-psychotic-junkies/. Accessed 19 Dec. 2016.

35 "TV networks load up on commercials - LA Times." 12 May. 2014, http://www.latimes.com/entertainment/envelope/cotown/la-et-ct-nielsen-advertising-study-20140510-story.html. Accessed 19 Dec. 2016.

36 "US Adults Spend 5.5 Hours with Video Content Each Day - eMarketer." 16 Apr. 2015, https://www.emarketer.com/Article/US-Adults-Spend-55-Hours-with-Video-Content-Each-Day/1012362. Accessed 19 Dec. 2016.

and break the mind-numbing effect that TV has on many people. If TV becomes a crutch and distraction from play, social engagement, and school, then limits should be enforced.

If TV is a must, a good rule of thumb would be five shows a week, period. That could be watched all at once or across each day. Also be aware of other screens: TVs in cars, videos on iPhones and tablets, etc. These add up easily and are just as harmful.

OUR SCREEN TIME

Technology is addictive. Literally, your body releases a happy hormone (called serotonin) every time you see a new message light or status update "like" from a social network[37]. While your child will grow up in a heavily digital world that we can only dream about, the relationship we keep with our devices and those we care about in person is a major lesson. If the fire alarm goes off, do you grab your child or phone first?

As a parent, we must be the first to show that we can put our devices down. This demonstrates our priority and how we live with these constantly present electronics. A good father I got to observe handled the following situation:

> (Thanksgiving dinner and the family is about to eat when the phone rings)
>
> **Kid 1**: Dad, your phone is going off.
> **Kid 2**: I know it was your phone because it went through the speaker.
> **Kid 1**: Want me to get it for you?
> **Father**: No, I have spoken to everyone whom I need to speak to.

---

37 Kent C. Berridge and Terry E. Robinson, What is the role of dopamine in reward: hedonic impact, reward learning, or incentive salience?: Brain Research Reviews, 28, 1998. 309–369..

I think many of us would have handled this differently depending on the dinner night, stress in our life, comfort at a quiet family dinner table, and such... Honestly, I have found myself tempted to grab a phone to "save" a situation, but we must prioritize our children first. Finding balance is necessary between our family, health, work, friends, and spiritual needs. As you find your balance, please consider that your family, health, friends, and spirit are harmed irrevocably if not given the care they deserve. If you leave your job tomorrow, in almost all cases, the business and customers will be served. If your family loses you tomorrow, the course of many lives will be deeply affected. The former CEO of Coca Cola has such a realization, and shared it at a Georgia Tech commencement speech[38]:

> "Imagine life as a game in which you are juggling some five balls in the air. You name them – **work, family, health, friends,** and **spirit,** and you're keeping all of these in the air.
>
> You will soon understand that work is a rubber ball. If you drop it, it will bounce back.
>
> But the other four Balls – **family, health, friends,** and **spirit** – **are made of glass**. If you drop one of these; they will be irrevocably scuffed, marked, nicked, damaged or even shattered. They will never be the same. You must understand that and strive for it."
>
> - Bryan Dyson – Former CEO of Coca Cola

As a busy parent and technologist, I always believed I could multi-task. Working on two devices or three at a time made sense to for me to being more productive, and certainly holding a conversation while

---

38 "ss - SMARTech Home - Georgia Tech." 30 Sep. 1991, https://smartech.gatech. edu/bitstream/handle/1853/41404/1991-09-30_17_27.pdf. Accessed 19 Dec. 2016.

checking email was normal. I was mistaken. Unfortunately, this isn't true for anyone and is actually detrimental to the tasks and harmful to the people (read: your child) involved. Simply stated, multitasking productively does not exist[39]. Study after study have shown that we, humans, perform poorly when we multi-task[40] (in fact, those who consider themselves GOOD at multi-tasking performed the worst of test groups). A hard fact, but in order to be a great parent, cease the splitting of your attention and give authentically to both your child and your work—just one at a time.

SCREEN TIME

While we have highlighted the scientific studies linking the use of screens (TV, tablets, smartphones, etc.) to detrimental effects in early childhood, in later childhood, and in creating adult disorders and diseases, there remains value in incremental usage of these devices. A lot of fun and creativity can be gleaned from these electronics, and proficiency in them is a requirement starting in middle school across many states in the U.S. Screen time totals should be inclusive of all of these types of devices, regardless of where they are used, or who the primary person is holding that device[41].

---

39 "Multitasking: Switching costs - American Psychological Association." http://www.apa.org/research/action/multitask.aspx. Accessed 7 Dec. 2016.

40 Sanbonmatsu DM, Strayer DL, Medeiros-Ward N, Watson JM (2013) Who Multi-Tasks and Why? Multi-Tasking Ability, Perceived Multi-Tasking Ability, Impulsivity, and Sensation Seeking. PLoS ONE 8(1): e54402. doi:10.1371/journal.pone.0054402

41 "Kids And Screen Time: A Peek At Upcoming Guidance : NPR Ed : NPR." 6 Jan. 2016, http://www.npr.org/sections/ed/2016/01/06/461920593/kids-and-screen-time-a-peek-at-upcoming-guidance. Accessed 7 Dec. 2016.

HOW MUCH TIME IS IDEAL ON DEVICE?

- Zero time on devices age 0-4
- 5-10 minutes a day on device 4-7
- 10-30 minutes a day on device age 7-10
- 30-60 minutes a day on device age 10-13
- Teenage years tend to be family unique

You'll note these times differ slightly from the American Academy of Pediatrics, as this includes parental habits and they consider screen time to include all screens (television as well as devices and we have broken them apart to match our daily reality)[42][43]. A recommendation from the AAP though that does add clarity for us parents is that we must "prioritize creative, unplugged playtime for infants and toddlers."[44]

When screen time is allowed, use this time to enable your child to self-manage their use of these devices. By programming the device (Kindles do this easily)[45], you can set timers on things like games, videos, and reading, and then allow your child to decide when and how to use their allotted time[46]. This is a powerful option as it empowers

42 "Children and Adolescents and Digital Media | From the ... - Pediatrics." http://pediatrics.aappublications.org/content/early/2016/10/19/peds.2016-2593. Accessed 7 Dec. 2016.

43 "The Impact of Social Media on Children, Adolescents, and Families ...." http://pediatrics.aappublications.org/content/127/4/800. Accessed 7 Dec. 2016.

44 "American Academy of Pediatrics Announces New ... - AAP.org." 21 Oct. 2016, https://www.aap.org/en-us/about-the-aap/aap-press-room/Pages/American-Academy-of-Pediatrics-Announces-New-Recommendations-for-Childrens-Media-Use.aspx. Accessed 13 Dec. 2016.

45 "Amazon.com Help: Set Daily Goals and Time Limits." https://www.amazon.com/gp/help/customer/display.html?nodeId=201730170. Accessed 10 Dec. 2016.

46 "How to Turn Your Kindle Fire Into a Totally Kid-Friendly Tablet with ...." 26 Dec. 2013, http://www.howtogeek.com/178303/how-to-turn-your-kindle-fire-into-a-totally-kid-friendly-tablet-with-freetime/. Accessed 10 Dec. 2016.

your child with choice, time management, and it requires zero effort from you. To be effective, you must enforce the timers and do not create an exception.

WHAT TYPE OF APPLICATIONS SHOULD I BUY/ALLOW?

- Encourage—Art, drawing, building interfaces - great for all ages
- Encourage—Gamified programming language apps
- Encourage—School education apps
- Avoid—In game advertisements
- Avoid—Videos, movies, or passive consumption
- Avoid—Apps that allow messaging beyond local friend circle
- Avoid—Apps that have content posted without filter (such as YouTube, Instagram)

It is absolutely critical to establish trust with devices. You won't always know who your daughter is talking to online. You won't know what your son is watching on YouTube in his room at night. Therefore, at the onset, we as parents need to establish trust with them and the devices. Setting the tone that they can ask you anything, about anything, and that their use of the device is their right to lose will pay massive dividends.

Trust but verify is an important assurance for you to establish with your child. In the early years of devices that can be accomplished by practicing any of these habits:

- All devices charge downstairs at night
- No locked/passcodes on phone
- Parent freely can use their device (for a quick picture, internet search, anything)

There may come a time when trouble is brewing with friends, the school, or warning signs from your child are emerging. While this is typically past the age of nine, you may need to be more vigilant and involved in the technology. Parents can add software that shares all the content on the device and other invasive methods to provide deep monitoring. These put at risk the trust you have built, but if safety is at risk it can be required.

Limiting the use of the screen time is to create many opportunities for our children, but there are additional serious considerations:

- Sexual predators used social media and messaging to identify and assault children 82% and 87% respectively
- Uncurtailed, kids spend 4+ hours a day passively looking at screens, and this increases to nearly 7 hours by 13 years old
- A recent theory on weak U.S. productivity is that there may be a link for productive creativity, activity, and execution with adult 'screen time' usage

The rule is they have to read more than they play video games"[47]

- Elon Musk for his kids

VIDEO GAMES

Our generation grew up enjoying video games, and now we are entering a time with even greater leaps in experience to include virtual reality and augmented reality. While these are exciting, it is important to remember that these games are recreating the real world, and sometimes it is best for us and our kids to live in the real world. The games you choose to allow should be healthy; they should reinforce your beliefs, and offer the child to expand their mind and creativity.

Games that have you create, perform music concerts, dance, solve puzzles, and have characters interact with a 3D world are all good examples. If you encourage these types of games your child will develop a more inquisitive mind that is successful at any profession

---

47 Vance, Ashlee. Elon Musk: Tesla, SpaceX, and the Quest for a Fantastic Future. First edition. Ecco, an imprint of HarperCollins Publishers, 2015.

and pursuit in life. Take care and be cautious with violent games, and this we shall define as any game where you (the main character) are given a mission is to kill or maim other people, objects, or sentients. Simple, but given the popular push of gaming to simulate war, anarchy, murder, and worse, you'll have your work cut out for you when your child comes back to the real world.

Play games for enjoyment and celebrate the exciting, fake worlds. Do not use video games as replacement of family time, social interactions, false parenting, or a means of distracting the kids. Typically the most important moments (social interactions, family time, "distracting the kids") are the most significant ones that'll develop your child's character.

Musk's rule for his own kids creates some adversity and require games that are not mindless

"They might have a little adversity at school, but these days schools are so protective," he said. "If you call someone a name, you get sent home. When I was going to school, if they punched you and there was no blood, it was like, 'Whatever. Shake it off.' Even if there was a little blood, but not a lot, it was fine."

What do I do? Create artificial adversity?

The biggest battle I have is restricting their video game time because they want to play all the time. The rule is they have to read more than they play video games. They also can't play completely stupid video games.

POSTURE—HOW IT EMPOWERS AND HARMS

There is a good deal of research in the field of psychology on how our emotions and feelings are displayed physically[48]. When we are happy, we smile, when we are sad, we slouch, and so on for other body language norms[49].

The reverse is also proving to be true. If we sit up tall, smile, and stand proudly, then we feel more happy and most significantly, we interpret our surroundings more positively. Unfortunately, when you observe how children use these "smart devices" (smartphones and tablets for instance), you can observe poor postures that can embed negative emotions and weak character conditions.

Imagine watching a football team leaving the stadium after being crushed by the other opponent. You'll observe their heads hanging low, forward, and between the shoulders. This is called the 'turtle effect," explained by nonverbal communication expert Joe Navarro, and this body language reflects the emotions of defeat and low confidence. Now remember the last group of kids you saw on these devices (at a bus stop, sitting at a restaurant, in a car), and you'll recall the exact same posture[50].

While we wait on science to prove it, we parents can act on these observations. As parents, we can help by instructing good posture, removing these negative postures, and thereby removing the negative mindsets associated with them. There is also research on powerful "confidence postures," the most popular of which is provided by social

---

48   Strack, F., Martin, L. L., & Stepper, S. (1988). Inhibiting and Facilitating Conditions of the Human Smile: A Non obtrusive Test of the Facial Feedback Hypothesis. Journal of Personality and Social Psychology, 54 (5), 768-777..

49   "Embodied Cognition A Comprehensive Summary – Why You Are Not ...." 30 Jun. 2014, http://bodylanguageproject.com/articles/embodied-cognition-a-comprehensive-summary-why-you-are-not-just-your-brain/. Accessed 11 Dec. 2016.

50   "Joe Navarro Books." http://www.jnforensics.com/books. Accessed 11 Dec. 2016.

psychologist Amy Cudy[51]. In this confidence posture research, Amy highlights that short periods of time in a particular position has a demonstrated perceived improvement on confidence. Sometimes that little edge of confidence is all that is required for our children to try something fresh and different.

51   "The Benefit of Power Posing Before a High ... - Harvard University." https://dash.harvard.edu/bitstream/handle/1/9547823/13-027.pdf?sequence=1. Accessed 16 Dec. 2016.

Saving your house from destruction

As you welcome your child into your home and he grows up, there will be a joyous amount of exploration, experiences, and play. There is one truth that comes along with these experiences—all the falls, misses, mistakes, flying toys, high speed chases, spills, pours, certainly lots of Picasso moments on any fixed surface, and in some cases the family pet. These are all to be taken with a good heart and cherished, they really are funny moments (sometimes later, much later). You can enjoy these with a bit of planning ahead and a bit of mental preparedness. Here are some ideas that have proven their weight in gold.

A few facts to be aware of are the acute differences between boys and girls:

- Boys = heavy running; high energy; lots of things of will become projectiles; strong chance of destruction. You'll want to really establish play areas and lock down the rest.
- Girls = light running; quickness; few projectiles; lots of mimicking of adult use of "things" (brushes, coasters, phones). You'll do best to provide her with duplicates or safe options.

HEIGHT IS YOUR ADVANTAGE

As your child grows, their reach and ability to disrupt your home will increase. Thankfully, we are taller, and can and should move at-risk items out of their range. The intent here is simply to encourage safe space to play. It'll lower your anxiety (from these items falling on child and from the child breaking that vase), and it'll enable you to allow independent play of your child (which will be a blessing as you'll be happy for a break here and there).

Now the run of conventional wisdom states that it is a good idea to raise anything that will fall and create anxiety out of your child's current reach, plus the height of your child if he were to stand on a stool. Place some items in cabinets and electronic wires tied up. You'll need to adjust this over time, but this approach is not hard, and further allows you, the adult, to still enjoy these items.

HOUSE SAVING IDEAS

"Tell me what I need in my house!"
"Why didn't you tell me that before?"
—Family and friend common asks

After much experimenting and messy lessons learned, here are a collection of the greatest house saving tips broken up in categories:

CREATIVE/TOY ROOM

- Dry erase markers & washable crayons—OMG, get them and you are welcome
- Painting your kids room? Use Eggshell/Satin/semi-gloss as these are very durable and you can easily wipe/wash it clean
- Set up an easel or simply a whiteboard for your child to draw on (easels are better because you can add a paper roll that costs $8 and lasts for about two years)
- Add a protective non-acidic sheet under the "art" area to capture any possible spills
- Pad the floors—yard sale purchase those puzzle padding or grab the ones I have on Amazon (this will save your floor as your child redecorates the room, drops themselves and other items on the floor, and save your floor from wear and tear generally)
- A smock for you and possibly your child
- Lots of drawers and shelves that are anchored to the wall

BEDROOM

- Add an extra bed liner on your child's bed until at least 4 years old (under the bed cover)
- Peel away stickers—Fun, independent play approved, and easy to remove!

CAR/TRAVEL

- Have a "go" bag in the car to include (keep in trunk and use/replace as appropriate (this saved me dozens of times):
- toilet paper
- a few Band-Aids
- a spare outfit (top to bottom)
- Handy wipe ($1 size)
- Neosporin
- small hand towel
- A few napkins
- Food - Applesauce pack and a granola bar
- Juice box
- Under car seat, add a leather/plastic pad—this will limit grooves and damage to car (I like the Brica)
- Add a pouch behind the seat to prevent feet hitting your seat and gain extra storage!

GENERAL HOME

- Don't have a nice thing where the child will be eating/playing on (such as thick shag carpet that will forever hide old food, and sticky treats)
- Sharp corners of furniture—covered to limit emergency room visits, with boys usually
- Electrical sockets—hard to connect the circuit but kids will figure it out
- Locked doors—have your interior door key ready (you know that little hole on the door), or rig the door so it cannot lock. This is a lifesaver for bathrooms.
- Anchor bookshelves to the wall with anchor bolts. This will save a doctor's visit as your little one works to stand up and perhaps when they try to climb

Bargaining the present for the future

Please cherish these moments with your child. Here is your chance to be curious and experience the miracle of life first-hand. Every day, your child will change and experience the world just a little bit deeper as he grows. In fact your child will double in size, weight, brain neurons, muscle, learn at least one language, learn to crawl, walk, run, swim, bike, jump, balance, and become proficient at reading, writing, and an abundance of other life milestones in less than 3 years.

In the beginning though, your child will first learn to see, and then after several weeks of seeing just you, he or she will see the world. The first time your child touches, tastes, smells, or sees something is the first time and only time that'll ever happen in their life. You get to be a part of that life, if you choose to do so with intention. We as parents can get wrapped up and so, here are a few reminders where we tend to miss the moment:

- At birth: we mistake the shortest of times awake as less valuable use of our time compared to other activities
- Breakfast: setting your alarm just 15 minutes early will remove the hustle and missed moments in the morning and start the day together
- Evenings: the time we enter the home till when our child is asleep is shorter than some commutes we make each day. Yet we unwittingly drive in silence and take calls at home
- Vacations: we create a work environment where we believe we cannot be gone. Maybe for Pope Francis or President Barack Obama that is true, but not for us

TAKE TIME OFF AT BIRTH

Most companies allow for 4+ weeks off after the birth of your child, and there are some rare ones that give a ton more to both the mother and father. You must take the MAXIMUM time off allowed, and actually take it. I know many who also use their short term disability to gain a bit more time. While the early months are mostly sleeping and eating moments, they are really hard mentally and emotionally. In addition, this is critical time where your child develops attachment and connects with the parents, so be present, both of you, and take the journey together—you'll be stronger as a result.

A great recommendation shared by others was to work from home at a reduced workload for the first 30-45 days, and then trigger the maternity/paternity leave and short-term disability. This allows for maximum bonding with your newborn and a balance of household + professional world.

ACTUALLY TAKE TIME OFF

If you don't value your time then nobody will, ever. How easy is it to say no to things? Not easy at all. As of late, our whole culture has been built around pleasing others and not saying no. It is helpful to know that this isn't the best way to live—nor is it the most productive. In fact, many time management and executive coaches encourage you to say no more often than not. They successfully take "real" vacations—meaning, vacations in which work is not present—and authentically connect with their passions and loved ones.

The difference between successful people and very successful people is that very successful people say "no" to almost everything.
—Warren Buffett

You must draw hard lines in the sand, and coming from the wrong side of this lesson, I cannot emphasize enough that you must defend your time off. That means when the day's work is done—it is done and you are with your family. When you commit to your family, it is as fixed as any client commitment on your calendar. When you go on vacation—you actually are on vacation, both mentally and physically.

Your family will recognize your love and passion for them, and it'll transfer both to personal experiences and professional. Here are a few tips to help in those hard moments:

- Add a block of time on your work calendar for your kid's activities
- Add travel time TO your kid/family event on your work calendar, this way you ensure you arrive on-time. Don't be that person.
- Leave the phone in the car every now and then (at the park, at the pool, while out to dinner, etc.)
- Block calendar for vacation in advance as busy; Set auto-email responder for all emails on how to proceed without you (do not say "will check emails at night")
- Don't actually check your emails while on vacation—try to NEVER read anything on your phone
- Try to NEVER speak on your phone regarding work related matters, and you know the call is about vacation if you can hand that phone to your child to speak to the caller

Protecting committed personal time and actually being on vacation is scary, I know—but trust me, if there is a REAL emergency, your team will find you. If they cannot survive without you, I recommend checking out the 4-hour Work Week by Tim Ferriss for tips to develop your team to be more independent. It'll change your life!

PARENT'S PERSPECTIVE

Family at kid concert
All "saving the moment"

CHILD'S PERSPECTIVE

Only "devices" -
no emotional connection,
no faces, no eyes, no smiles

LIVE LIFE ACTUALLY

Are you engaged in the experience, activity, or event with your family and child? Or, are you finding yourself viewing life through the view-finder/smartphone screen watching a 2D version of life happening in front of you? (For example: filming her performance instead of watching; "Live streaming" an event for your social media page) Please don't be these things, for the sake of your child.

Excuses and logical arguments aside, reflect on the fact that you are physically there, but only seeing it on that flat screen. It doesn't matter that you want to capture the moment, that you want to live stream it for family in Africa, or any other reason. All of those needs can be addressed with a fixed tripod or paying someone to make the recording for you. You see, this isn't living life actually. You are watching life and have forgotten the whole point of being present: your child.

What is your child seeing? NOTHING but a bunch of faces covered with phones. No smiles, no eyes to connect with from the stage, and occasionally a flash to tell them the audience is out there, somewhere. When you record this way—YOU are not authentically connecting, and how brave your child is to be on stage to perform, and to have no warm smile of appreciation to reciprocate with and build confidence upon.

Live actually and you'll have all the memories that matter.

CHAPTER 7

"YOU JUST WAIT…" IT'LL BE HARD, THEY SAY

THE "DIFFERENT ISN'T HARD" CHAPTER:
- ✓ What is hard
- ✓ Everything is awesome
- ✓ Enjoy the process
- ✓ Shifting your mindset

What a terrible thing for parents to tell future parents, but I hear it nonstop. I heard it before I became a proud father, and I have heard it dozens of times since from other parents. Even worse, these naysayers continue their comments year after year, since they just made it through that age/period and only recall the bad. Let's put an end to that with an important shift of our own mental state.

We are raising a child, and each moment in life is a gift. We get to feed him/her late at night when they awake from a peaceful sleep. We get to change their diapers promptly to keep them clean, healthy, and comfortable. As they grow and begin learning logic, good vs bad, and what is allowed, we get to teach them. We have the privilege in this relationship, every step of the way, to be a trusted loved one in their journey of life.

Is it hard? Some moments are difficult, sure. These are temporary and passing. Are we scared? Sure. Do we get mad, angry, exhausted, and confused? Yes. It is not the challenge, but what is important is how you react to it.

For your child's health, be the best you can in each moment, and that will be perfect.

THERE
ARE
SOME
THINGS
MONEY
CANNOT BUY, LIKE

1. MANNERS
2. MORALS
3. CHARACTER

What is hard

HARD IS OUR PERCEPTION OF CONTINUALLY HAVING TO RELEARN HOW TO BE A PARENT.

When we frame it this way, it makes more sense and is approachable. As new parents, there is a continual learning curve, because just as we get a handle on say, changing diapers, we are potty training. Just when we find the perfect way to entertain our newborn, they are crawling around and pulling on the drapes. This nonstop change will encompass everything from their playing, eating, sleeping, speaking, and all the wonderful new experiences of life. This is them growing up, so enjoy the change and the opportunity to learn new skills with your child.

"YOUR LIFE WILL NEVER BE THE SAME."

Well obviously, since now we have a third, fourth, or fifth entirely new human in our house that wasn't present a few weeks, months, or years ago. Who we are as people doesn't change because we are parents, nor does how we interact with the world change. Now we balance our child's needs with exposing them to the world as we see it. Life doesn't stop, but it's more like we operate on an access road for short bit of time.

"GET YOUR SLEEP NOW!"

There is quite a bit of excitement when your child is home with you, and frankly, in the beginning that natural response is worth its weight in gold. You'll want to be attentive and responsive day and night. Most of the sleep we lose is due to our own accord. We sleep with one eye open and two ears pointed towards our baby's room. Naturally, we will be more tired—we are half asleep for the first few months!

This isn't hard, but uncomfortable. You'll need to adjust your day-time activities to reflect the stress you are experiencing and change in sleep patterns. Most find it very helpful to grab a 20-40 minute nap in the afternoon (if you are at home) or right after work. It is important to schedule this with your spouse so you both get these power naps, as this will raise both your ability to enjoy each other and the baby's time.

As you move into the toddler and later years, you'll have more and more sleep with surprise nights. Those nights may be simple potty accidents, fevers, colds, nightmares, or any sort of thing. Comfort them and care for them without frustration. You can do it, and the better you manage the moment, the swifter it'll pass without drama.

Parents tend to actually be more tired in the toddler years as the child is just getting really mobile, and usually the parents are a bit tense. If you create the play spaces discussed earlier, your stress should be significantly below that of the average parent's. Your ability to establish a routine of time daily with your family and kids will allow for you to be engaged and a part of your child's life. Scheduling can be tricky, but ever so important. In fact, Elon Musk, founder of PayPal, Tesla Motors and SpaceX makes it home for family dinner and brings his children on trips as their schedule allows. If he can manage this, we can do it too[52].

---

52   Vance, Ashlee. Elon Musk: Tesla, SpaceX, and the Quest for a Fantastic Future. First edition. Ecco, an imprint of HarperCollins

What to expect at each stage

The physical changes in early childhood are dwarfed by the leaps and bounds your child's cognitive and language development. As you experience each of these classic stages of growth, enjoy the process because they are short lived. It is absolutely amazing when we pause and realize how far and fast your child is developing.

From the moment your child is born, they are learning from the environment using every one of their senses. They are developing a sense of cause and effect, and they are tuned into how you as the parent respond. Your every physical, emotional, verbal, and nonverbal responses are being measured, adapted, and mimicked. What an exciting and terrifying reality!

INFANT

"Hold onto your butts", in our best *Jurassic Park* reenactment. Out of the gate, your child and you will be adapting to a new world. You will be experimenting on finding what is best, and most likely your child will focus on sleeping, eating, and...well, pooping. This period may seem just primed physical development and survival, but is actually the critical time where emotional development is formed.

There is a good deal of research around attachment theory that your child's individual differences later in life and personality are shaped by the caregivers in this first year. This attachment can impact all future professional and personal relationships. Needless to say, this is why your active and authentic presence is so critical.

You will be in a whole new world. It is exciting and terrifying all at once. When you bring home your baby, you don't know a lot of the unique characteristics about your child, and that is OK—they don't know either! You'll both discover these through experimentation and patience. Other parents will give ideas on what has worked, and you'll find some are more effective than others. Just prepare yourself for the unknowns. A few key unknowns that we as parents do not know on day one:

- Their personality
- How they like to be put to sleep
- How they like to play
- If they like to be held
- What toys will they enjoy
- Will they like swinging or not

You will figure these out together, because when you think about it, you don't know, your child doesn't know, and you will learn to read their comfort and discomfort as the only real way of knowing in the beginning.

There are constant questions with a baby. You'll have to feel out your baby to learn their tolerance for discomfort, and thus your need to be reactive. Your pediatrician will meet with you several times in the first few months, which are great for reassurance and question moments. Finally the few big areas you need to keep an eye include—eating, pooping, sleeping, and fevers. These little ones need your utmost attention and protection from the elements at this early stage. A rich website with detail for all parents of infants is kellymom.com. Detailed articles and discussions that can show parents in similar situations for little ones. In addition, the smartphone app Wonder Weeks gives you detail and insight on the (mental) leaps and bounds of your baby.

WHAT TO EXPECT:
- Child will develop emotional connections with present caregivers (who is raising your kid?)
- Motor and basic skill development
- Growth stats: 2x Height, 4x Weight
- Language usage with vocabulary of 300-1,000 words

FUN AND CHALLENGES:
- Matching games (sound & object association games)
- Reading and storytelling (lots of your voice and direct contact)

Parent Thinking 101 on how to know when to react with a "sick" baby

How do you know if your baby is sick or not sick? Is that something we should worry about at this moment? How do we know? Here is the thinking of a great parent (who is also a nurse) on how she approaches such a scenario:

"My baby has a cough. Do I worry about it? With a baby I worry, but not as much as my toddler. As a toddler I know more—I can tell when something is BAD for her or bad for the baby. Little babies can turn very fast when something is wrong. An older kid has a greater reserve and tolerance based on vaccinations and their immune system in general. Fever, personality changes, sleep changes +/-.

If I am unsure, I call the nurseline (or Pediatric nurse) after checking my baby's temperature.

TODDLER

Your typical toddler has mastered many skills, including sitting, walking, potty training, using a spoon, scribbling, and sufficient hand-eye coordination to catch and throw. This also where the "terrible twos" happen. Taking it from the child's perspective, this is them seeking out the edge of what is allowed. They are still bundles of raw emotion and respond in sometimes powerful demonstrations (temper tantrums). You need to be strong in these formative years. Your little one now has independence and is exerting their own free will[53]. As the parent, you must show paths that are allowed and certainly those that are not.

The parents who navigate this age best are crisp in what is allowed and not to their children. They direct their children to realize and rationalize what is appropriate behavior. These parents are unyielding

---

53   "Stages of Growth Child Development - Early Childhood (Birth to Eight ...."
http://education.stateuniversity.com/pages/1826/Child-Development-Stages-Growth.html. Accessed 19 Dec. 2016.

but kind in their parenting. You'll sometimes have a raging, yes raging, child that you'll need to forcibly remove from a room, house, and environment. Other times you'll see your child rattle between different ranges of emotion.

At this age, you'll also be the target, and victim if you aren't prepared, of "test" temper tantrums. These are situations in which your child will literally be faking it to test your reactions and moral flexibility. Here you need to balance being attentive, responsive, caring, and parental such that you don't become a helicopter parent yielding to a two year old's whims.

At this age they are starving for friendship, they want to be friends, and they are heavy with emotion and unsure how to handle it. They love exploring their world, everything is new, and they are constantly asking questions. "Why this?" "Why that?" "Why why why!" This is when you are teaching the most as parent. They are learning everything. Enjoy!

WHAT TO EXPECT:
- Potty training (not an overnight event and accidents happen, so be prepared to minimize discomfort)
- Raw emotional responses
- Scribbling, coloring, and lots of experimentation with colors on all surfaces
- Peer relationship development, gender identification, and right and wrong (as you have defined it)
- Language usage with vocabulary of ~1,500 words

FUN AND CHALLENGES:
- More complex matching games (word & object association games)
- Lots of reading and storytelling
- Playing catch with all manner of objects
- Drawing animals, shapes, and coloring
- Making paintings

- Tea parties
- Soldiers, toys, dolls, and deep imagination play
- Visit the library
- Silly putty
- Cut paper for an hour and glue

EARLY CHILDHOOD

Here is where your child becomes active and starts participating in 'regular life' activities. This is a super fun and intense age. They'll have fine motor skills that allow running, jumping, balance, and gymnastics to become more fluid. Their precision with writing, drawing, and cutting will also improve[54].

Here is a great age to really engage them in the arts, piano (fun), musical instruments, and lots of playground areas. The more canvases and experiences you can expose them to here, the better. This is also a time for having your child be part of the family through chores, activities, and such. These can include tasks as simple as holding their own umbrellas, handling dishes to the sink, finding/folding their clothes, helping make dinner, etc.

In this age you'll also tackle, what appears, to be selfish behaviors. At this age your child really hasn't developed a perspective for another individual, and therefore the concept of sharing is foreign. Be patient, be fair, and just know this is a mental concept that is developed—not automatically and not overnight.

You'll also begin to see important social relationships develop in this age, and it is critical for these to develop. This will define how your child relates to people and peers throughout their life.

WHAT TO EXPECT:
- Friends, best friends, and the formation of relationships

---

54   "Child Development & Early Childhood Development Advice . PBS ...." http://www.pbs.org/parents/child-development/. Accessed 19 Dec. 2016.

- Ability to pick up complex hand, feet, and body movements (dancing, karate, gymnastics, diving/pool tricks)
- No training wheels and full speed ahead down hills
- Greater body strength and the use of strength in competitive fields (ropes courses and such)

FUN AND CHALLENGES:

- Card games, Uno, and board games where rules are increasingly complex
- "Chapter" books like Charlotte's Web and even their own creation of art books and story books
- Playing catch with all manner of objects
- Nerf gun wars
- Building obstacle courses with physical challenges
- Ice skating
- Kickball games
- Flying kites

STAGES
Childhood & Activities

Toddler
Ages: 1 - 3

Early Childhood
Ages: 3 - 8

Infant
Ages: 0 - 1

Shifting your mindset

How you perceive and approach each day will define if that day is hard or enjoyable. Consider how lucky you are to have this little one in your life. How much it is a privilege and not a right. Life is a miracle and many would give their left arms to be in your position! You are a very lucky couple.

There are methods and practices you can undertake to actively shift your mindset. Embrace these and seek out your own too.

YOU 'GET TO'

Being a parent gives you millions of moments to care for your child. You get to be a role model, a caregiver, a teacher, an impromptu doctor, and a dozen other specialties. Despite where you fall on these skills, you are the best and most important person in their life. These are not requirements or a job, but a chance for you to give your best.

When you find yourself in challenged moments, reframe the task from 'a have to' into 'a get to'.

Advocating Opportunity	Parenting Move
Change her diaper in middle of night	Make her comfortable and rock to
Drive him to practice	Be with him to prepare his mind for practice
Give a bath	Play and share water fun and keep him healthy

Turn every "have-to" into "get-to". You don't have to go to work. You don't have to go grocery shopping. You don't have to pick up the kids from soccer practice. You GET TO do those things. Flex your gratitude muscles by recognizing the abundance and opportunities in your life.

Ben Bergeron, Coach to Fittest Athletes in the world

DON'T COMPLAIN

Sure, some things are gross, inconvenient, and tough, but don't complain—ever. Complaining only breeds more complaining and negativity. You'll need to find ways to do better, of course, and those must certainly be thought out with your spouse and family, but avoid complaining about the activity. Instead find ways to make the activity better, less gross, and better for your child and for you.

When we complain, others want to jump on the "complain train." This is creates an atmosphere and tone that will be felt by your child. In addition, activities that you may have been neutral on will now become a negative, as you allowed yourself to be reframed.

Cherish and seek out the best you can in each moment. Don't complain, don't reciprocate complaints, and I promise those 2:00 A.M. diaper explosions will have more comedy than horror.

FIND THE FUN

There is a great deal of funny moments—day and night that happens with raising a child. Have fun! Enjoy yourself! Actively find the fun, the enjoyable, and reflect this positive energy.

Something magical happens when you are positive—your child connects with that energy and reciprocates. Nothing better than a distraught child that is scared suddenly being wrapped in warm arms that are positively giving love vs. an angry parent flustered with being awoken in the evening. Also, recall that your child is learning cause and effect, right and wrong, and how you react to certain situations will dictate how the child will react when they happen again.

There is nothing wrong with you enjoying raising a child. You can be happy to do all the day-to-day activities and the extraordinary efforts too. Nobody should sway you any other way. If you hesitate, ask yourself this: are you afraid you'll make others feel bad? Do you feel guilty for enjoying what others are struggling?

This is nonsense, and you shouldn't fall into this downward spiral simply out of caution for others. No, you can help change their perspective, and if not, simply know they are in a tough place.

CHAPTER 8

PREPARING FOR THOSE 2:00 AM MOMENTS AND EXCELLING

HEALTH AND LATE MOMENT MASTERY TIPS:

✓ Medical essentials for infant, toddler, and early childhood years

This chapter is dedicated to arming you for the 2:00 A.M. moments with the hard earned lessons of others. This is not a complete list, but contains the most significant ones based on parent feedback. It is important to have at least these resources at the ready, and to keep your kit current and fresh. It is not ideal to visit a 24 hour pharmacy at 2:00 A.M. while your child suffers at home. Logistically, it is very hard, and emotionally, it is exhausting beyond description.

Having these key items and information on hand will certainly make daytime first aid simpler too.

YES, I KNOW
IT IS 2:00AM
BUT I
THOUGHT WE
COULD
HANDLE THIS

COLD, RASH, NOW
ITCH, FEVER

Medical essentials in first few years

So what do you need? Well, it all depends on where you live, and frankly, what works depends on your personal body chemistry. The following is what has worked for others, but please check with your doctor first, read the labels, and know this isn't meant as medical advice but instead observations from other parents.

Now what you'll need for a situation will vary, but based on the type of situation, medicine, remedies, and ideas have been shared below. In the beginning, your child will have more discomforts than real infections/bugs, so it is more a pursuit of remedying these discomforts. Remember, they DID just enter the world, and their skin, eyes, ears, and all have never used or exposed to the outside world before, so there is an adjustment.

INFANT

Your little one is experiencing our world all at once, in all its rawness. The air quality, dryness, temperature, oils from people, new surfaces, light hitting their eyes, sounds now crisper to their ears, and a million other sensations are affecting their body all at once. On the opposite side of the spectrum, your child will be exposed to very few people and therefore few colds and bugs, and with the pediatric sequence of vaccinations these lifesaving medicines will help keep your child healthy (Fun fact: our medicine has reduced child mortality rates from about 35% to near 5% globally!)

Here are ideas and methods that have helped others ease their child into our world.

GENERAL TIP FOR PARENT:
• Ear thermometer

HEAD:
- Cough suppressant —Humidifier + "vaporizing steam liquid"
- Cough suppressant - Medicated vaporizing chest rub (life saver!)
- Ear Drops
- Coughing - Delsym (infant)
- Dry/Stuffy noses - gentle moisturizer - saline nasal spray

BUTT & PRIVATES:
- Butt Rash Cream - A+D zinc oxide cream (prevention + just a little red irritation relief)
- Butt Rash Ointment - A+D (helps heal dry & chafed skin)
- Diaper edges to prevent heat & skin irritation - Burt's Bee's Dusting Powder (talc free)

SKIN:
- Natural oils
- Mittens for their hands (early days)
- Lotion - Burt's Bee's lotion
- Rash/Eczema - Aquafor (red checks)

INTERNALS:
- Gas discomfort, caused by swallowing or certain foods - Mylicon gas relief

PREPS:
- Phone number to nearest pharmacy, plus pharmacy's operating hours
- Emergency room contact information & address in your phone
- Phone number for poison control
- First Aid kit in car

TODDLER

Your little one is likely now in some daycare or kindergarten and exposed to families of all backgrounds. While this is beautiful for social development and convenient for working parents, it is a pure breeding ground for colds, rashes, infections, and bugs. It is during this time when your child will get sicker than any other, and you will too.

It'll be your duty to care heavily for yourself and your child, as the colds they pick up at school will spread like wildfire through your home. This all will pass, but be prepared and persevere through it with a positive attitude. Take care to allow these to work themselves out whenever possible, allowing your toddler's body to be challenged by these infections will strengthen their immune systems. Overmedicating has become a common mistake, and while antibiotics are effective, they have their specific and limited value.

GENERAL TIP FOR PARENT:
- DO NOT finish your child's food, ever.
- Don't share silverware, ever. If you must taste the food, do it first, and then allow them.
- Colds/infections require more attention, as conditions can change quickly for a small child. Things to keep on the lookout to help you read these "tea leaves":
  - » Fever
  - » Personality changes
  - » Sleeping changes (more or less)

HEAD:
- Cough suppressant - Humidifier + "vaporizing steam liquid)
- Coughing - Delsym (children)
- Ear Drops
- Dry/Stuffy noses - gentle moisturizer - Saline Nasal Spray
- Common cold, flu, sore throat, headache, toothache, fever - Children's Motrin (Ibuprofen)

- Pain reliever/Fever reducer - Acetaminophen

BUTT & PRIVATES:
- Butt Rash Cream - A+D zinc oxide cream (prevention + just a little red irritation relief)
- Butt Rash Ointment - A+D (helps heal dry & chafed skin)
- Diaper edges to prevent heat & skin irritation - Burt's Bee's Dusting Powder (talc free)

SKIN:
- Lotion - Burt's Bee's lotion
- Neosporin
- Anti-itch cream for bug bites

INTERNALS:
  GasEx
- Pepto Bismol liquid

PREPS:
- Phone number to nearest pharmacy, plus pharmacy's operating hours
- Emergency room contact information & address in your phone
- First Aid kit in car (refresh the neosporin spray and resupply Band-Aids)

EARLY CHILDHOOD
Prepare yourself, as soon as your child spends 4+ hours a day with non-family members (think daycare and school), a full assortment of colds and ills are highly likely. Ones you'll see most common are strep, pink eye, and plenty of stomach aches. You'll have to balance caring for

the symptoms and allowing their body to develop antibodies. There is also a psychological balance where you'll be teaching you child how to deal with these discomforts, and knowing where they cannot.

If your child has been through daycare, kindergarten, and such then colds here should be rare. You'll have annual allergy possibilities and of course flu season, which is usually easy to address with an annual vaccine. Toddler advice and ideas are shared below, and tend to be more familiar to adult medicine and remedies.

HEAD:
- Coughing - Delsym (children)
- Cold & Flu - Children's Dimetapp Cold & Cough Daytime and Nighttime
- Cough suppressant & nasal decongestant - Muscinex (Very Berry is my child's favorite)
- Ibuprofen + Acetaminophen

SKIN:
- Neosporin
- Acne - Coconut oil charcoal soap

INTERNALS:
- Pepto Bismol chewable

PREPS:
- Phone number to nearest pharmacy, plus pharmacy's operating hours
- Emergency room contact information & address in your phone
- First Aid kit in car (bigger band aids, maybe some medical wrap, bee sting ointment)
- Poison Control phone number

CHAPTER 9
STRONG BODY; STRONG MIND

HEALTH AND WELLNESS CHAPTER:
- ✓ How did nature intend us to eat?
- ✓ Sugar, Fat, Portions, Treats
- ✓ Strength solves many problems

Your child can only make good choices on food if you have prepared them with being familiar and comfortable with how certain foods make them feel. How they eat for their entire life is defined by how you set them up through early childhood. As they grow to age 5 and enter school they'll have freedom to eat whatever they desire. Your lack of control on his or her eating will rapidly increase, and that freedom is supported by your demonstration at home.

Allow your child to develop good taste, comfort in food, and aware-ness of its effect on them. Ellyn Satter, a pioneer in raising young eaters, makes the division of responsibility around mealtimes easy - parents provide the **what**, **where**, and **when** and your child decides the **if** and **how much**[55]. A simple concept combined with making only 1 meal for the family, a practice all great parents followed. The

---

55   "Division of Responsibility in Feeding - Ellyn Satter Institute." http://ellynsatterinstitute.org/dor/divisionofresponsibilityinfeeding.php. Accessed 19 Dec. 2016.

information in this chapter is shared to empower you and give you the best tools for making decisions in your own home.

Recognizable food = Richer nutrients

Simple Guide to Good Health:

- Select only real food
- Eat in a structured way that matches nature
- No label reading, because real food has none

How did nature intend?

What is good food? How should we decide what is the right amount and type of food to provide that supports the development of our child, and perhaps give ourselves a few extra years of enjoyable living? While this is an ever deep, and controversial topic, there are a few mainstays that appear self-evident that should guide our hands.

One positive and reassurance to the parents is that your child will not allow itself to starve. There will be times when your kid will be too full, or not in the mood to eat. That is OK. If they choose to skip a meal and make it up (or learn a lesson if it was a mistake), all will be fine.

HOW TO PICK OUT THE RIGHT FOOD

Naturally grown food is the best food and thankfully it is the simplest to purchase (usually grocery stores place these on the edges of the store). There are no labels to chase down and you don't need to have a degree in science to know what is in that steak, tomato, or pile of almonds. So how we define good food can be simplified to meet the following general characteristics:

- No sugar, (aka: corn syrup, high fructose, aspartame, sucralose)
- Not created in a factory (No processed, packaged, or constructed food)
- Grown or raised (plant or animal) - primary source of all nutrients
- Unprocessed food = good fiber, great fat, minerals, and rich vitamins

Food that falls in line with the above are the best ingredients for your meals. If you combine these foods in a balanced manner that fits your lifestyle, you'll be well suited for all the adventures your little one pursues.

NUTRITION, AS NATURE INTENDED AT BIRTH

We can choose to eat anything we want, any portion, and adjust the macronutrients (protein, fat, and carbohydrate amounts) as much as our heart desires. This isn't true for any other creature on our planet. We have philosophies that encourage a plant based diet, others that recommend grains as a major part of your diet (U.S. recommendation since the early 1970s), and a few that are more fat-based (Atkins[56] and Paleo)[57]. Note the breakdown in the chart are approximate average figures, as each eating style either listed a range or stages to follow, or both.

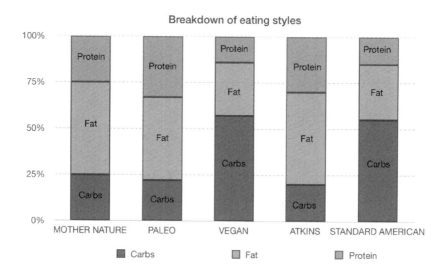

Thankfully, we as parents and our infants do not have to worry about the latest diet fads or tinkering in their food makeup. The best balance of nutrients is provided naturally from a mother's breast milk. Infants can be fed up to 2 years in this manner, being supplied all the nutrition they will need. Most interesting here is how Mother

---

56 "Scientific Research - Page 1 | Atkins." https://www.atkins.com/how-it-works/library/articles/scientific-research. Accessed 15 Dec. 2016.

57 "2015-2020 Dietary Guidelines for Americans - Health.gov." https://health.gov/dietaryguidelines/2015/resources/2015-2020_dietary_guidelines.pdf. Accessed 15 Dec. 2016.

Nature distributes these macronutrients[58], and perhaps how can we as parents apply this wisdom to our child's diets as they move on to real food:

- 10-20% Protein
- 50% Fats
- 25-40% Carbohydrate

Nature intended humans to live off a diet consisting of these macronutrients at the earliest age. Of course some migration is expected and you need to adjust how you feel, how your child feels, and how we perform in our lives.

It is important to highlight that additional benefits are achieved from real food (unprocessed) as is provided in breast milk. Babies receive rich minerals, vitamins, and foundational components through breast milk (highlighted in the box).

Human milk composition provides the standard for human infant nutrition that safeguards infant growth and development. Highlights of some of these components are highlighted here[59]:

- bioactive factors
- cells (growth regulating hormones, metabolism, T-cells, stem cells)
- anti-infectious and anti-inflammatory agents,
- growth factors (support intestinal tract, vasculature, nervous system, and endocrine system),
- prebiotics

Our challenge as parents is to ensure that when we transfer our children off of breast milk to common food, which we try to stay true to these food distributions and rich vitamin & mineral sources.

---

58 "PubMed Central, Table 1: Pediatr Clin North Am. 2013 Feb; 60 ... - NCBI." https://www.ncbi.nlm.nih.gov/pmc/articles/PMC3586783/table/T1/. Accessed 19 Dec. 2016.

59 "Human Milk Composition: Nutrients and Bioactive Factors - NCBI." https://www.ncbi.nlm.nih.gov/pmc/articles/PMC3586783/. Accessed 19 Dec. 2016.

> ## Case Example: When a 5 year old makes a lunch of carbs & candy
>
> "Our kids (ages 5 and 13) pack their own lunches. If they choose to have no sandwich, they have no sandwich.
>
> I taught them what is enough food and what should be included, but I am not there to babysit everything they do. They have to learn. They have to make bad choices. We all learn from failure, and if we never let them fail, they will never recover.
>
> One day, Flynn (age 5) packed his lunch for the next day. He had a yogurt, a bag of chips, and 3 pieces of candy. The next day Flynn went to school, and by that afternoon he was a jerk, hungry, and a complete butthead. 'I am starving.' I asked him, 'Why did you have that?' and then, 'How do you feel?'"

The case example above lessons were numerous and powerful for all of the boys. The big boys recognized their importance in being a family unit, Flynn never packed a bad meal since, and everyone learned the importance of helping people who need help.

BUST THE MYTH, FAT IS GOOD

Mother Nature provides babies with nearly 50% (in fact, nearly all mammals on earth consume milk with this fat content) fat as part of their early diet. A clear intuitive signal to us that fat is good and can be embraced. Here is a simple rule:

> *Natural, nature-made fats are good
> vs. Artificial, manmade fats are bad*

Avocados, nuts, olive oil, and even the fat on steaks and lard are re-establishing themselves as better alternatives than factory made 'fat free' solutions. (For example: an average steak has both good and bad fats, but the proportion of good outweighs the bad.)

Fat is also a slow-burning fuel for the human body and has sticking power that sugary carbohydrates do not provide to the body. All in all, it is better to ensure we serve a portion with every meal to keep our child running strong and growing tall.

SUGAR

If there is one thing as a parent to avoid, this is it. Sugar by any name that is attached to it does violent things to the biochemical world of our body. Study after study prove that sugar impacts social behavior, mood, ability to focus, energy levels, and can be attributed to dozens of social dysfunctions. One study from UC San Francisco even found that drinking sugary drinks like soda can age your body on a cellular level. Even more scary is the idea that by us, the parents, serving our children these sugary foods and beverages we are actually building an addictive habit. As parents, we can avoid that by limiting sugar, period.

"Evidence supports the theory that, in some circumstances, intermittent access to sugar can lead to behavior and neurochemical changes that resemble the effects of a substance of abuse... defined by tests for bingeing, withdrawal, craving and cross-sensitization to amphetamine and alcohol[60]"

This isn't easy in our society. Manufactured food is stacked with sugar and the television blasts four hours a week of advertisements at children convincing the subconscious it needs these "treats."

---

60   Avena, Rada, and Hoebel. "Evidence for Sugar Addiction: Behavioral and Neurochemical Effects of Intermittent, Excessive Sugar Intake." Neuroscience and biobehavioral reviews 32.1 (2008): 20–39. PMC. Web. 15 Dec. 2016.

Sugar cube content for common items in our lives

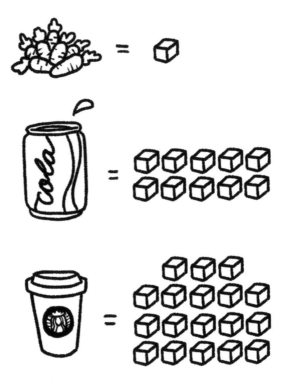

Parents prevent these hazards to their children by limiting this negative ingredient, and we can do so by first eliminating sugary beverages (i.e., zero soda, sports drinks) and this will eliminate nearly a third of the sugar. The next most effective action is to avoid processed foods. That'll eliminate the surprise sugar ingredients. The next time your child needs to replenish their energies give them fruit, fruit packs, and similar foods. The fiber will help satisfy their hunger and the fruit will super charge them for more activity.

Sugar goes by many names, here are a few favorites on labels to help you in the grocery store: Acesulfame potassium, Aspartame,

Neotame, Saccharin, Sucralose, and Advantame[61]. These sound natural and delicious, right?

Our generation invented and updated common foods with increased carbs and sugar (through factories we created "low fat" foods), based on the nutritional guidance that was reinforced in America since the late 1970s. We greatly increased the consumption of carbs and decreased our fat calories on a percentage of our diet (directly going against Mother Nature's distribution). Since this adjustment we have increased carbohydrates from grains annually nearly 60 pounds a person and caloric sweeteners (primarily high-fructose corn syrup) by 30 pounds, according to the U.S.D.A. agricultural economist Judith Putnam[62].

This trend also matches up to the obesity, diabetes, and heart disease trends in the same period. There is correlation and our scientists are just now recognizing the connection, though it is against the mainstream view.

PORTIONS

You as the parent need to set meals that include good options. In the beginning you'll be leading the effort to build their plates, but quickly your child will be able to take the lead. Great parents create options for their kids, set the table (or off the counter in many cases) and allow the child to place food on their plate. Your child gets the choice and building on the guidance you have set forward in the years prior, plus your own plate as an example. Your child will eat as much as they require, and if you don't allow meal replacing snacks, they will eat all required at these times.

---

61   "Artificial sweeteners - Mayo Clinic." http://www.mayoclinic.org/healthy-lifestyle/nutrition-and-healthy-eating/in-depth/artificial-sweeteners/art-20046936. Accessed 19 Dec. 2016.

62   "Abstract - Economic Research Service - US Department of Agriculture." https://www.ers.usda.gov/webdocs/publications/sb965/14812_sb965_1_.pdf. Accessed 15 Dec. 2016.

A simple rule of thumb for guiding portion sizes of food is easily described as follows[63]:

- **Make a fist** - put that much protein (meat/fish) on your plate
- **Turn hand over, make a cup** - put that much fat on your plate
- **Fill** the rest with vegetables

As your child grows, the portions grow at each meal, so everything is proportional. Note: there is zero place for grains in this approach. These should be rare and far between. Good examples of when grains and fruits should be eaten is around physical activity (karate, gymnastics, track and field, kickball), as these foods instantly spike the blood sugar levels and will facilitate the quick energy recharge necessary, and provide immediate help to the recovering muscles.

TREATS AND TIMING

Providing nutrition to your child is both a physical task and a mental effort. The sections up to now have focused on the physical task—what kind of food, how should you portion the food, etc. The other side of this coin is mental, and that relates to the psychology of making food a reward system or demonizing certain types of food. These are subtle challenges for you as the parent, and will greatly affect your child as they develop in life.

As you raise your child, the first thing is never to criticize/ridicule/ or chastise another person for what they eat. Your child will see, hear, and process that internally. Equally, you must never demonize a type of food (in the same sense that we must not demonize drug use). It has been well proven that when something is denied a person—they tend to attract to it more strongly.

Instead, focus on the positives of how food makes someone feel,

---

63   "On Twinkies, Cigarettes and Reason by Dan Edelman - CrossFit Journal." 30 Oct. 2012, http://journal.crossfit.com/2012/10/on-twinkies-cigarettes-and-reason.tpl. Accessed 15 Dec. 2016.

how the protein will make them stronger, and any other associations you like on a positive nature. Positive reinforcement is significantly better than being negative to a type of food. A good example is the case study with Flynn our 5 year old above.

An easy method of balancing the frequency and celebration of treats is to create simple groupings. Each grouping provides a frequency and shows where food lands. That way your child knows they can always eat certain foods as hunger requires, and treats, candy, etc. are reserved for rare moments. This also will help eliminate the grocery store candy aisle raids that seem hardwired into many kids.

- All-the-time foods:
  » All of our "good food"
  » Meats and veggies
  » Sometime foods:
  » Fruits, Nuts
- Rare Foods:
  » Cake, Candy (i.e., sugar-based)

As we associate rare foods to events—birthday parties, Thanksgiving, and such, we encourage the enjoyment and social togetherness. We also can use these as personal observation moments to see how our child reacts during and after such sugar. A common occurrence is the child feels ill/crazy/tired afterwards, and these are good moments to ask how they feel, and why they think they feel that way. Most children easily connect how it was the sugar. Now they have a negative cause and effect feeling to that food, and it truly becomes a treat with an accepted cost. A common tip shared during interviews included the parent feeding their child a healthy snack or meal before such celebrations. This way the child had some good nutrients in their body before the party began.

Strength solves many problems

How your child builds their body, develops their functions—minor and major motor skills, and builds richer neurological trained skills like coordination, balance, agility, and accuracy is fueled by the food provided. After you have provided the energy for development, it is time to use those creative free play spaces. Allow your child to learn to trust their legs, their grip, their aim, and then to test yours by running, biking, and leaping in the air. Children are amazing, and they take time to blossom into who they will become, both physically and mentally.

There will be many "day ones" and your child will look to you for help at becoming proficient at each activity. You will need to learn to coach, instruct, be a safety net ("spotting"), and demonstrator of these activities. One area you can influence and support is for them to build a base of strength that will protect their bodies as they test their limits, but also enable them that first successful step.

These experimentations and development across these two domains (motor skills and neurological development) will feed naturally into their academic pursuits, thereby instilling confidence and self-awareness on completing activities to hit their own goals. It doesn't matter whether their life goals are going to Mars as a space pilot, or simply being the lead scientist in their third grade class—having these traits will help, no matter what their aspirations entail.

KIDS BUILD STRENGTH BY BEING KIDS

It is amazing to watch kids, exhausting some would say! They move constantly. It is their natural response to be active to climb, dig, and soar as far as possible. As your little one continues to grow into the toddler years, you have a chance to introduce him/her to many physical activities. These are games, jungle gyms, monkey bars, slides, and more. Nature provides us with trails to hike, rocks to climb, rivers to cross and paddle, and more.

The more you do, involve, and enjoy as a family unit the stronger and more confident your child will become. This strength will then transfer to classic sports and athletic abilities later in life.

A magical thing happens at playgrounds once a kid has mastered a certain apparatus (swing, climbing wall, monkey bars). They make it more difficult. Where they used to walk up stairs, now they climb. Now they run between objects. Now they jump off of swings. The football tosses are just a bit farther. There is massive entertainment and opportunity in these common places, but under the surface your child is growing stronger.

Children from infant up to early childhood don't need treadmills, gym memberships, or anything. Kids up to pre-teen are extremely active and have shortened school class schedules (so less sedentary forced periods), but teens and up definitely benefit from more protected time for play, and that may be a planned exercise that they enjoy. The key for parents is to be sure your child has these physical times to have fun, and all the while appreciate they are getting stronger and more resilient to injury/broken bones. Trust that through this physical exploration of the world, they will be more capable to pursue their next *big hairy audacious goal*, as made popular by James Collins and Jerry Porras.

A powerful example is found with Serena Williams, who began passionately playing tennis at the age of four, and became one of the greatest tennis players ever and more so when paired with her equally successful sister, Venus[64]. She pursued goals has continued with her sister, to be one of the best in the world.

Your son or daughter has the strength and potential to become anything they want. The only limits are those we artificially place upon them, and at these ages there should be no limits. Whether their moment of passion is space flight, or an athletic discipline, or even wizardry when it comes to cooking—we can stoke that passion and fire. We can introduce them to the excitement they envision through

---

64 "About Serena - Serena Williams." http://serenawilliams.com/about/. Accessed 13 Dec. 2016.

play and direct experience. Shed the baggage of the prior generation and pass on the insights you have to help them grow their future.

You don't become what you want,
you become what you believe
- Oprah Winfrey

CHAPTER 10

CONCLUSION

"THE FIRST DECADE" CHAPTER:
- ✓ Let your child teach you
- ✓ Be prepared
- ✓ Uncharted territory

Great parents think like you and I, and in fact we each have the means, motivation, and aspiration for our children to be great parents. As we highlighted across these chapters, there is a balance and flow that exists between each parent and child. No child or situation is the same, so there is no absolute checklist or task list. If there was such a list, surely we would find ways to bring it to the masses. There isn't, and therefore we have highlighted the activities, thinking, and methods of great parents here in this book so they can be adapted to your own family.

We have the privilege to raise a child—each moment given to us in this experience is a gift. Those moments together make up the personality, opportunity made available to the child, and their view of the world for the rest of their life. This is such a privilege, but also the most significant act many of us will ever share with the world. In fact, your child will be on Earth (or Mars if Elon Musk continues on his path) at least 50 years longer than you and I. Amazing to think of it in that manner.

This chapter will recap a few key concepts shared within the text, and will arm you for the first ten years of your child's life. The following chapter includes valuable challenges and games that you can try to realize the concepts in this book directly in your life!

Two of the greatest gifts we can give our children are roots and wings

- Unknown

Let your child teach you

"It'll be hard" they say—so what! Enjoy the process and every moment. Each change from infant to toddler and to early childhood will be awesome. Each activity is a chance for you to be together, experience life through their eyes, and perhaps learn from your child. I find it incredible and wonderful the number of parents whose own personality has transformed after their child has entered into early childhood.

The parents themselves are learning from the child. They are re-learning the amazing surprises, beauty, adventure, and fun that exists in every moment. Whether it is make believe with a cardboard box (that has become a spaceship), or cushions that are a fort, or maybe how simple and fun a few pebbles discovered in the yard might be to fresh eyes.

Seek out opportunities for your child to teach you. These are not actual lessons (though your 6 year old will love playing school with YOU being the student), but lessons of emotion, observation, and visual creation—all of which are non-materialistic and fantastic. You'll grow and benefit in the following areas, if you let your child take you there with them:

- Simple beauty (e.g., crystals in rocks)
- Tastes (e.g., lemons)
- Empathy (e.g., caring for stuffed animals and others by playing doctor)
- Joy (e.g., true laughter)

Your children are actually smarter than you think they are. The way children think is brilliant. If you can follow their train of thinking, it is so simple and all that is necessary. This communication and learning is a two way street.

You must learn to let go. Learn and appreciate that you cannot and need not control everything. Learn to let your children do things— even if it isn't the way you would do it. You must remember and learn to think before you react and talk, because your children are learning and watching your behavior. It is the little things that they are learning, and it is your opportunity to create caring, thoughtful, compassionate, and loving kids.

We are all human

Society places artificial limits on what should be a character trait, a skill, strength, or a weakness. Furthermore, it imposes goals upon our children. Your child is first and foremost a human, and second, a boy or girl. The only limits, fears, and stigmas you place on your child are your own doing. The same is true with unlimited potential for greatness, pursuing "big hairy audacious goals," and learning love. As the parent, you have the chance to encourage the positives and limitless potential. Those who strive for greatness will have failure, but those failures will certainly be beyond those who never attempted. Enjoy the process your child will discover and experience as they move through some failures and most certainly, success.

> *The most certain way to succeed is just to*
> *try one more time*
> Thomas Edison

We must each teach our girls and boys to be leaders, to stand up for what is right, to defend themselves and others. Encourage singular focus on excellence in all that they choose to do. Embrace for your child all that can be dreamed, for it is only the limits of our dreams that should guide our child's future. Elon Musk looks at the world now and envisions us on Mars. Oprah created from nothing a media empire that has brought incredible opportunity. Katrin has gone from crumbling in competition to besting every woman in the world TWICE, and maybe a third time as this is published.

Seizing and challenging life by overcoming failure, which is the skill we need to promote for all children, boy and girl.

Be prepared

Great parents set up their child's environments for success. They don't control the activity, as independence is better learned even if it requires a few band aids or washing away paint. We've highlighted how you can prepare creative spaces that keep your home intact and stimulate the most creative inspirations from your child. In addition, there is tremendous importance in supporting your child's development and proficiency in artistic and sporty activities.

The benefits of being prepared extend to being aware of the growth of your child, the changes they'll experience, and the adjustments you'll make in your parenting approach. The transformation and growth from infant and toddler as a single example are dramatic, and include everything from a full change in the food they eat to how they play, sleep, speak, and explore their emotional faculties. The transition in this period physically is also spectacular, as they go from not moving much to running, jumping, and more! Be ready to adjust and be present, because the moments will tick by very quickly.

Seek out friends and family to support you. While you CAN do it all alone, there is a benefit to having a support structure. Everyone wants to help and many will not put their hands forward without your offering. Those who have healthy kids are great partners in raising your child. For friends and relatives it is best to gradually build trust and experience. They will appreciate the gentle learning curve and honor your trust.

Uncharted territory

You will find yourself in new experiences, challenged with fresh questions, and you'll need to do many things you have zero knowledge about. These can be minor and intense, but all surmountable by you, with your support team, and the riches of the internet. You see, there is no other choice. You are the parent and your child has the fullest of faith in your capabilities. Moments may not be great, and mistakes happen, but that is the process. Learn, move on, and apply that new knowledge. How you handle the good, bad, and unknown is a key attribute of great parents. You can do it!

Your path and the course you create for your child will be unique and reflective of their needs, as well as your ability to respond. Armed with the hundreds of habits, methods, and attitudes of great parents, you are well prepared—now more than ever. You and your child have the freedom to pursue your own path and not one that mimics popular media or that of the classic Joneses. It is your chance to make "a different road" that matches you and your child's abilities, as reflected on by Serena Williams from her own childhood and tennis[65].

THE FIRST 10 YEARS, AND THEN...

This book certainly does not have all the answers, and I have myself have regrets. I have made mistakes and I can only pray that my efforts place my own daughter and our children on a healthy path in life. We cannot control the flow of life, but we can make the most of the moments we have together, and as parents we GET TO set up these situations in the most impactful manner.

For the first ten years of life, we have shared here the ways great parents think and how they set themselves up for success. What happens after those early childhood years is a personal adventure and for another book. If you see your daughter or son pursuing and

---

65   Edmonson, 2005, Venus and Serena Williams, pp. 46–47.

experimenting in entrepreneurial activities, Raising an Entrepreneur: 10 Rules for Nurturing Risk Takers, Problem Solvers, and Change Makers by Margot Bisnow is insightful and can help you steer them along. As your child blossoms into their own person, your continued demonstration of excellence and passionate pursuit of the highest aspirations will continue these great lessons.

You have the skills, knowledge, and appreciation by now to give them the best opportunity. Be optimistic, have confidence, and work through the challenges with your child together. This focus on preparation and process will prepare them for a life full of unknowns and beautiful challenges.

They are little humans, so treat them like it

Holly J.

ADDITIONAL ACTIVITIES AND BIOS

"FUN AND EXPERIENCES" CHAPTER:
   ✓ Activities to authentically connect from great parents around the world
   ✓ Luminary Bios

Everything is new to your child. Every moment, every taste, every sunset, every bird, every rock, and every light. How wonderful that you get to experience this newness with them. Throughout this book, we highlighted the ideas, habits, thinking, and practices of great parents. In addition, research from professionals dedicated to the field of infant and early childhood was incorporated, but there is more.

You can experience many of these moments with your child. You can use directed play, create scenarios, and or simply make it possible for learning and growth to happen. These are highlighted within this chapter as challenges for you. They require your effort, sure, but honestly, they are adventures and games to your child. This isn't work, but does require effort that'll realize much joy for you and your child, together. Remember, you GET TO do these, and they will further cement your bond.

Additional activities to authentically connect

Below are shared activities from a wide range of great parents and literature. Enjoy, customize, and make these your own.

CHALLENGES FOR TODDLERS/EARLY CHILDHOOD
- "Grown up play"
- Make breakfast with your daughter/son - mess be damned
- Seriously, have the toddler mix something, break some eggs, measure ingredients
- Full tilt tea time - water and little mini scones that you bought the night before
- Build cities, houses, forts out of everything - Legos, couch cushions, umbrellas, old boxes, or even Jenga blocks
- Play school; school bus; and camp
- Make a music or dance performance - give them noisemakers, blinking lights, and allow for the performance
- Are you repairing a household appliance or maybe fixing a hole in the wall? Any house repairs where you can show and share in the process of repairing is very enriching for kids - let them participate!

"MOVE TOGETHER"
- Go ice skating or roller skating - year round!
- Headstands (against a couch) are the first step to freestanding handstands (for you and your child!)
- Yoga - do yoga at home welcome them to join (remember passion first before precision)
- Training/Fitness - if you do it, your child will appreciate it (so take them with you when you train, CrossFit, weightlift, etc.)
- Fly kites in the park, in the yard, down the street!
- Running - take your infant/toddler in a stroller for a run or bike ride

- Go bike riding to a park or at a park (as early as 2.5 years old)
- Pools, lakes, oceans, or even simple sprinklers in the yard - get in, get wet, and have fun
- Dance - boys and girls enjoy it equally. Classic music, oldies, Disney tunes, and more. Join in, dance together, dance solo, but dance - no spectating
- Play catch - boy and girl. Inside, outside, and with anything (toys, stuffies, glitter covered fluffy balls, tennis balls, and anything else
- Get on and enjoy Jungle gyms, monkey bars, and rock climbing. Then get out of the way and let her discover and play

"DISCOVER"

- Paper airplanes - out the window
- Show rockets launching into space (Can't get anywhere fancy? Go on YouTube and then go outside and show where they went.)
- Show stars using star viewing iPhone/Android apps and let your child explore
- Go outside - collect rocks, collect feathers, have a small picnic with a Reese's cup, etc...
- Just get the kids outside - enjoy the trails and the simple things.
  - » Explore and go, complaining be damned.
  - » Teach the process on how to solve and figure out wilderness with a dying phone and compasses.
- Finger paint, melt crayons on paper, grab a roll of paper and make anything (ideas: animals, a farm, hot air balloons)
- Find trees and climb them together
- Walk along creeks, hop rocks, and look for nature
- Get on a farm visit the animals, feed some, work on the farm, and bring to life the words of their books
- Horseback riding - even the smallest of ponies will make for a great experience. As your child gets older, you'll be able to join equally
- Read books to each other - about animals, the stars, the oceans, super heroes, and even the Princesses

FANTASTIC RESOURCES AND IDEAS FOR ACTIVITIES:

- Pinterest (men and women check it out!) has a ton of crafty, seasonal, and free ideas
- Target $1 section
- Michael's Craft store - they typically have little projects for <$4 that'll result in at least an hour of fun
- Parks and outdoors - jump, climb, and enjoy (always a winner)

BOOKS TO STUDY, SCAN, AND ADD TO YOUR KNOWLEDGE:

- Books for you:
- Wherever You Go There You Are, by Jon Kabat Zinn (Mindfulness)
- Mindful Parenting, by Jon Kabat Zinn (Mindfulness)
- How to Raise an Adult, Julie Lythcott-Haims (Preventing over parenting)
- PDF of Ellyn Satter's Division of Responsibility in Feeding: http://ellynsatterinstitute.org/cms-assets/documents/203702-180136.dor-2015-2.pdf

BOOKS FOR YOU AND YOUR CHILD:

- *Imaginations: Fun Relaxation Stories and Meditations for Kids*, by Carolyn Clarke
- *Don't Let the Pigeon Drive the Bus!*, by Willems, Mo
- *What Do You Do With an Idea?*, by Kobi Yamada and Mae Besom

Luminary Biographies

ELON MUSK:

Elon Reeve Musk was born in 1971 in South Africa and moved to the west when he was 17, primarily to avoid being placed in the military and supporting apartheid. His current ventures and business pursuits include: SpaceX, PayPal, Tesla Motors, Hyperloop, SolarCity, and OpenAI. He also has six sons: Nevada, Griffin, Xavier, Damian, Saxon, and Kai.

Elon has a brother (Kimbal) and sister (Tosca). He was raised between his mother and father, Maye and Errol Musk.[66]

KATRIN TANJA DAVÍÐSDÓTTIR:

Katrin, born in Iceland, grew up as a gymnast. Around 2012, Katrin entered the competitive scene of CrossFit at the elite level. She placed 30th and 24th in 2012 and 2013 respectively. In 2014, Katrin missed qualifying for the CrossFit Games, and refocused with her coach Ben Bergeron on closing her weaknesses—specifically building her mental strength and strengthening a few specific fitness areas[67].

Then in 2015 and 2016, Katrin won the CrossFit Games back to back, a feat which was previously done by only one other woman. Katrin currently trains in New England with her coach[68].

---

66 "Elon Musk - Wikipedia." https://en.wikipedia.org/wiki/Elon_Musk. Accessed 15 Dec. 2016.

67 "Athlete: Katrin Tanja Davidsdottir | CrossFit Games." http://games.crossfit.com/athlete/55121. Accessed 15 Dec. 2016.

68 "Katrín Davíðsdóttir - Wikipedia." https://en.wikipedia.org/wiki/Katr%C3%ADn_Dav%C3%AD%C3%B0sd%C3%B3ttir. Accessed 15 Dec. 2016.

OPRAH WINFREY:

Oprah Winfrey (whose proper name is "Orpah") was born in 1954 in Mississippi to a poor family. Oprah persevered despite, by all accounts, an abusive, difficult, and tough upbringing. Her hard work and skills as an orator came through the first time she was on a microphone, and in her career, she has launched numerous TV shows and built a media empire[69]. Some highlights of her professional accomplishments include being the host of "The Oprah Winfrey Show," Chairwoman and CEO of Harpo Productions, Chairwoman, CEO, and CCO of the Oprah Winfrey Network. Additionally, she is a successful actress and author[70].

Oprah is an active philanthropist, speaker, and mentor to communities around the world.

SERENA WILLIAMS:

Born in the United States in 1981, Serena has been generally coached by her father Richard Williams since she was 4. She holds numerous accomplishments and distinctions, including winning the most major (Grand Slams) titles in singles, doubles, and mixed doubles amongst active players, male or female. At age 38, her major titles place her fourth on the all-time list[71]. While her prize money is impressive, totaling $81 million in 2016, more so is her individual match performances. Serena's win loss record is 775 wins to 129 losses (singles), and as of September 2016, she is ranked #1 in the world[72].

---

69 "Oprah Winfrey's Official Biography - Oprah.com." 17 May. 2011, http://www.oprah.com/pressroom/oprah-winfreys-official-biography. Accessed 15 Dec. 2016.

70 "Oprah Winfrey - Wikipedia." https://en.wikipedia.org/wiki/Oprah_Winfrey. Accessed 15 Dec. 2016.

71 "Serena Williams: Home." http://serenawilliams.com/. Accessed 15 Dec. 2016.

72 "Serena Williams - Wikipedia." https://en.wikipedia.org/wiki/Serena_Williams. Accessed 15 Dec. 2016.

INDEX

Smoking, 40
Son, 23-29, 31-35, 90, 135, 143
Sports, 56, 60, 70, 72, 75, 78, 79, 82, 85, 130
Sugar, 48-50, 123, 129-133

T
Tablets, 19, 33, 86, 88, 93
Teamwork, 56
Temper tantrums, 109, 110
Time, 4, 6, 11, 16-19, 33, 41, 52, 55, 67, 71, 86, 90, 98, 146
Toddler, 25, 39, 89, 106, 115, 119, 139, 146

V
Vacations, 47, 98-100

W
Winning, 30, 34, 60, 82
Winning isn't Normal, 82

ACKNOWLEDGMENTS

This book represents a lifetime of notes, research, experience, and discussions. As a father, son, uncle, and caregiver, through life I have many cherished moments, as well as acts that truly were life changing. At the same time, I have made many mistakes and seen the effects of such actions. If the reader is spared even just one of these moments of regret, this manuscript will be worth it. Over the past few years I have more so been blessed with learning from great parents from all walks of life. Parents with a single kid to parents with four of various ages and personalities. Parents in all income brackets, and from around the world. The commonality of shared love for their children resonated constantly in these parents, and it gives me great hope that our shared belief in a better future will allow us to create one for each generation forward.

Greatest of thanks is owed to Ma and Jeff for demonstrating so many amazing qualities as parents, adults, and supporters in all of life's adventures. The insights and habits shared throughout this manuscript are gathered from decades of observations and life moments, but there have been several key families, parents, and friends who contributed their valuable time and patience in this process directly.

My deepest thanks to Stacey Owens and her little dudes; Holly and Brian Johnston and their four boys supporting BullDawg nation; Dr. Jenn and Tym Kaywork; Callie and Drake for their examples around the power of mindfulness; Chris and Curt Disser, who demonstrate daily the value of independence, so much so that during our interview extra kids showed up to stay for dinner; Katie and Marc Chillion; Tarl Veal who has raised five amazing and happy children; Melissa Webb and the insights on 2 A.M. moments; and Catherine and Scott for acting as a sounding board in this experiment called parenting.

Special thanks is owed to the generous and extremely busy friends, professionals, and experts who reviewed, cut, corrected, changed, and honestly transformed the manuscript into the book shared today. While I cannot possibly name everyone and certainly there were many who in confidence and personal exchanges shared their insights, a few owe special thanks. My heartfelt thanks go to Dr. Jennifer Kaywork, Stacey Owens, Callie Green Van Fleit, Meghan O'Brien, Shaun Heneghan, and Laura Sikes.

Finally, a sincere thank you to all the parents who are seeking excellence for their children and working every day to make it happen. You are great role models and inspiration for each of us in our lonely moments. A special thanks to those who give me strength—Anna and Andrew Foard, Andrea and Andrew Esposito, Anneke Brandsma Smith, Michael Schneider, Jenny Dowd, Aimee and Brody Harris, Cathy Facer, Jill Johnson, Marsha and John Dickerson, Paula Molinari, Dan Ingevaldson, Clo Huyghues-Despointes, Michael Morales, Candace and Michael Cavan, Jason Smalls, Holy and Cole Erickson, Kristen and Michael Stainback, Jenny and Joe Astrauckas, Brittany and Brandon Markey, Ryan and Janelle Knight, and Adam Smith.

Writing a book isn't done in some far-off place. It is done at one's home, in coffee shops, and in every hour that can be stolen and saved. Thanks to all the proprietors, and establishments (such as Land of a Thousand Hills in Roswell GA, Octane Coffee on the West Side) for all their fine Wi-Fi, caffeine, and patience.

As I sit and write these last few words, I cannot express the joy I have had reliving past moments in my own life while my daughter sleeps nearby. She continually surprises me with her curiosity and love for the world. I hope this book serves new parents, like my life-long friend David P. Brown and his wife Kim Brown, and all parents across each stage of early childhood. It is because of my family and friends that I wrote this book to help.

ABOUT THE AUTHOR

James is a father, uncle, son, and caregiver with a daughter attending second grade. James professionally specializes in developing practical and elegant insights to highly complex situations in the technology and cyberspace field. These skills of pattern matching, observation, study, broad research domains, and experimentation bring a distinct set of skills to form these concrete examples and ideas around parenting.

He has worked and spoken at schools, community centers, and globally for the past 16 years on topics ranging from parenting tips for kids with technology to deep analysis on cybersecurity matters. James is a constant researcher and experiments personally on a field of topics including nutrition, fitness, automation, methods of communication, and leadership.

James is also passionate and deeply involved in the CrossFit community, the endurance athletic field (such as Ironman events), enjoys short day adventures in the mountains. He resides in Atlanta, GA.

James J. DeLuccia IV

Made in the USA
Columbia, SC
18 August 2019